MY JUPITER for PERSONAL GROWTH and PURPOSE

An Astrology Coaching Workbook

By Robin Wald

ISBN: 979-8-9877146-0-7 (Paperback)

Book design & formatting by Dominique Nieves.

To my parents, who fostered in
me a lifelong love of learning,
teaching and kindness

TABLE OF CONTENTS

Introduction

For many years I have known there are books in me waiting to be written. As a professional consulting astrologer, certified life coach, and spiritual teacher, I have varied but integrated areas of knowledge I feel called to share. A potential challenge of my Sun and Moon being in the fixed air sign of Aquarius is a tendency to get stuck in the ideation stage. Up to now, I struggled with committing to one topic or setting aside the time in my already full schedule to put pen to paper, fingers to keyboard, and to manifest the ideas in my head into the written word.

Part of the guidance I offer as an astrologer is to help clients tune into the current universal planetary energies and cycles interacting with their unique birth chart, so they can align with those energies for their highest good. Practicing for myself what I offer others, I am aware that this is an auspicious time for me to finally buckle down and write.

As I begin to write this on August 4, 2022, Mars is in a very rare triple conjunction with Uranus and the North Node in the earthy, productive sign of Taurus. Uranus, the modern ruling planet of my Aquarius Sun, Moon and Mercury, brings about sudden flashes of insight, change, and progress. Mars is the energy of fierce, bold, passionate action toward a desired goal. It is the fuel and fire to act now! The North Node beckons us to grow, challenge ourselves and evolve into who we are intended to become, however uncomfortable that may feel.

Saturn, the traditional ruler of Aquarius, and archetype of committed, persistent hard work towards a long-term goal, is currently in Aquarius nearing a conjunction to my natal Moon and Sun, inviting me to put in the disciplined time and effort to accomplish something I feel and know to be important to me.

Jupiter (as you will understand in way more depth as you move through this book), is the planet of expansion, growth, vision, faith, abundance, and possibility. After spending the last year in Pisces in my twelfth house and crossing my Ascendant, Jupiter is currently in Aries (initiating action) in my first house (identity and personal will). What a great time to act on my vision to write a book about Jupiter and its cycles!

Mars is also about to enter Gemini (the sign of communication, writing, teaching, learning) on August 20th for an extended seven-month period, through March 24, 2023. In my personal natal chart, this Mars transit is hitting my 3rd house of communication, writing, and teaching.

There is a lot more I could say about the cosmic synchronicities in my own journey at this time, **but this book is about YOU!**

<u>**Specifically, this book is intended to help you make sense of Jupiter in your own life experience**</u>:

- What does Jupiter in your natal chart show about your personal growth, soul purpose, and potential?
- How and where does Jupiter's energy of optimism, joy, and faith express itself in your life?
- What are your Jupiterian ideals, visions, and aspirations?
- What do Jupiter's twelve-year cycles reveal about your personal growth journey and evolution through different moments of your life?
- How might you intentionally align with Jupiter's cycles to manifest the abundance, wisdom, and success you seek and deserve?

My intention in writing this book is to create a very practical, accessible, hands-on workbook that you can use at your own pace, to help you get insight for yourself in a way that feels relevant and impactful for you. Whether you are brand new, intermediate, or advanced in your knowledge of astrology, this book will support you to understand Jupiter's potential in your chart and life.

By exploring Jupiter cycles, this book will help you create new awareness and insight about how you have grown and are continuing to grow in your aspirations, vision, values, faith, spiritual connection, and sense of purpose. Creating awareness is a foundation for making intentional, empowered choices. You can come back to this book year-to-year as Jupiter changes sign through the zodiac, to create awareness around how and where you are being called forth to grow and open yourself to new opportunities for abundance and blessing.

As a consulting astrologer, my role is to translate and interpret the complex mathematical, symbolic, and archetypal language of astrology into relatable language so my client can create meaning for themselves. As a professional life coach, I create a safe space in which clients can self-reflect about their wants, needs, vision, goals, challenges, possibilities, resourcefulness, and action steps. I ask powerful questions, listen deeply, and challenge people to transform their thinking, actions, and results. As a mindfulness and yoga teacher, intuitive Tarot reader and spiritual educator, I encourage people to compassionately trust in their own inner knowing and wisdom from an integrated place of mind, heart, body, and spirit.

My Jupiter for Personal Growth and Purpose: An Astrology Coaching Workbook is designed to give you direct access to these powerful modalities -- astrology, coaching, mindfulness, and intuition -- so you can explore and create empowered narratives about your past, present and future.

This book does not seek to be a beginner's primer on all things astrology, or to be an academic masterwork on the science and astrology of Jupiter. There are countless astrology books and online resources, beginner through advanced, that I am personally grateful for in my own learning and refer you to in the bibliography (Appendix A) if you feel called to further your learning.

<u>**Instead, what I am excited to offer you in this book is**</u>:

- A summary understanding of the astronomy and mythology relating to the planet Jupiter
- A personally relevant understanding of Jupiter's astrology in your birth chart that you can put into immediate use, whether you are a complete beginner or advanced student of astrology
- A summary understanding of the signs, houses, planets, and aspects to aid you in decoding how Jupiter operates for you in a given sign, house, and in relationship to other planets
- Practical insight into the potential of Jupiter in your natal chart, especially as it relates to your personal growth, life purpose and abundance
- Hands-on interactive worksheets with prompts and reflection questions to help you make meaning of Jupiterian themes in your life
- An exploration of Jupiter cycles as opportunities for personal growth at different key times throughout your life in the past and into the future
- Suggested practices informed by coaching, mindfulness and Tarot to help you access and trust your inner wisdom
- A safe place to create awareness and wisdom for yourself, and to support your journey forward in a way that is of highest benefit to you and the people and projects that matter to you

Chapter 1 – Jupiter in Astronomy, Myth, Archetype and Symbol

Jupiter is the most massive planet in our solar system. In fact, it is two and a half times the mass of all other planets in the solar system combined. Jupiter is known as a gas giant, with hydrogen and helium gases being its primary composition. The visible Giant Red Spot on its surface is a centuries-old storm bigger than Earth. The winds at Jupiter's surface create rainbow auroras. Doing everything on a grand scale, Jupiter has ninety-two known moons -- the most of any planet -- and that number keeps increasing thanks to the new NASA Webb telescope. If not for Jupiter's magneto-sphere guarding Earth from all manner of cosmic collision, our relatively tiny planet and all life we know on it would cease to exist. To see some images of jupiter check out NASA's website.

Jupiter's larger-than-life prominent role in our solar system is echoed in its mythological associations in the Earthly realm. Jupiter was aptly referred to by the Greek philosopher-astrologers as the "Greater Benefic," bestower of blessing, and was assigned as "ruler" of Sagittarius and Pisces, the signs associated with Divine law and transcendence.

Jupiter is named for Jove, the Roman sky god of thunder and lightning who was king over the other gods, and chief deity of the Roman Republic. His equivalent in Greek mythology is Zeus, God of the sky, thunder and lightning, and father of the entire Greek Pantheon of gods and goddesses on Mount Olympus. Zeus, who was the ultimate authority over Divine law and justice, was both magnanimous and prone to excesses, and his symbols are thunderbolts, rainbows, and eagles.

In Hebrew, the name for Jupiter is Tzedek, which translates as justice and righteousness, qualities associated with God and human potential. We see Jupiter's association with rainbows showing up in the Noah's ark story in the book of Genesis, when God sets the rainbow as a symbol of the promise to protect and never destroy life on earth again. Later in the Book of Exodus, when God enters into a covenant with the people at Sinai, God appears in a terrifying stormy display of thunder and lightning -- calling cards of Jupiter. A theme of the Old and New Testaments is that blessings are bestowed on those who align with a spiritual path.

In Hindu mythology, Jupiter is called Guru, or Devaguru, and is associated with the Lord Brihaspati, the divine spiritual teacher or priest who imparts wisdom and learning. The planet Guru reveals truths about light and dark, and about higher law and morality and is associated with blessing, luck, and prosperity. The Vedic god Indra, known as King of the Devas, is associated with the sky, thunder, rain, and lightning.

In Norse and Germanic mythology, Thor is the God

associated with the planet Jupiter. He is linked with thunder, rain, fertility and with the protection of humanity on the Earth. Thor is also the namesake of Thursday (Thor's day), the day "ruled" by Jupiter astrologically since ancient times. We also see Jupiter/Jove's influence in other languages' names for Thursday, with Jeudi in French, and Jueves in Spanish.

Jupiter's symbols

Bows, arrows, archers, thunderbolts, rainbows, heavens, sky, eagles, centaurs, horses

"The primary urge of Jupiter is to connect with something greater than itself." -- Steven Arroyo, Exploring Jupiter: The Astrological Key To Progress, Prosperity and Potential

The "glyph" or symbolic representation of Jupiter is a combination of a cross or plus sign, and a half-circle arc. The cross, with its x and y axis and four points, represents our physical experience of embodiment in the material world. The half circle represents our spiritual journey towards some higher connection, a yearning to be whole, to commune with Oneness which is symbolized by a completed circle. The placement of the half-circle balancing on the shoulder of the cross symbolically implies that our physical, bodily experience in this world is the "reality" and foundation from which we elevate, aspire and seek to become one with higher Truth and purpose, on a soul level.

> *"If Jupiter is to participate in the fulfillment of an individual's solar purpose, then its urge toward expansion must be channeled. This is stated symbolically by the Sagittarian archer who aims his arrow upward and thus gives a specific direction to the Jupiter energy." -- Alexander Ruperti, Cycles of Becoming, p.115*

Simply put, Jupiter urges us to grow and expand, especially on a soul level. Just as an archer aims her bow at a target, Jupiter in your chart aims your soul towards connecting with its highest purpose, ideals, vision, and potential. It has a future orientation, setting its aim on growing you towards a big, hopeful, optimistic vision of what is possible in your journey of becoming.

According to Arroyo, "*Growth* and *becoming* implicate the future, and probably nothing else in the birth chart is so closely related to future direction, aspirations, and plans as Jupiter. Its natal sign, house and aspects help us pinpoint areas of growth, rapid development, probable success, meaningful improvement, and expanded understanding." *Exploring Jupiter*, p. 6-7.

As a professional astrologer and coach, a very common issue clients come to me with is that they are seeking more meaning and purpose in their life. They want to feel more fulfilled, more inspired, and more aligned with something personally meaningful that energizes them into action each day, whether that be around career, relationships, or anything else.

<u>**Some questions clients ask me include**</u>:
- What am I really supposed to be doing with my life?
- What would make me really happy, that I might intentionally design my life around?
- Am I learning the lessons and growing in the ways I am supposed to be learning and growing?
- How can I use my unique gifts to benefit the world as well as my own abundance and success?
- How do I satisfy this yearning to feel deeply connected with my true self, with other people, and with the Divine/Infinite/God/Source?

Astrologically, the first planet I look to for clues to help someone answer these "big" questions is Jupiter. A person's Sun, Moon, Ascendant, North Node, Midheaven (MC), and other points in the chart complete the picture with key information, but Jupiter is the star at center stage.

Our contentment or discontent in our current reality is largely influenced by our perspective and beliefs. Neuro-scientists and psychologists assure us that our mental, emotional, and physical health are affected by what we tell ourselves and believe to be true. Beliefs matter -- especially our beliefs about what is or isn't possible in our life. **Jupiter guides us to believe in a higher ideal or future vision, and those ideals and visions inform the quality of how we live in the present moment.** Aspirational, faithful, open-minded beliefs about what is possible, can inspire us to grow, learn, and act in ways that move us forward towards success and fulfillment. But when our connection to higher ideals or soul purpose is challenged (which may be represented astrologically by a difficult Jupiter placement or transit), we may experience a crisis of meaning or lack of faith in what is possible. Pessimistic or close-minded beliefs can keep us stuck in inaction and unfulfilling patterns that limit our success and joy.

There are many coaching strategies that can help a person understand their "growth and becoming" such as powerful questioning, silence and spaciousness to reflect and respond, mind-body-spirit exercises, visioning exercises, identifying limiting thoughts and beliefs, identifying and developing resources, goal setting, and accountability. This book will integrate astrology with some of these coaching strategies to support your process of becoming more conscious and empowered around your personal growth and potential.

Let's start by understanding more about the key themes associated with Jupiter. Astrologically, this is referred to as a planet's "significations."

Jupiter Significations or Keywords		
Growth	Faith	Joy/Joviality
Expansion	Spirituality	Abundance
Ideals	Philosophy	Optimism
Vision	Possibility	Aspiration
Purpose	Adventure	Potential
Meaning	Generosity	Opportunity
Boundlessness	Truth	Prosperity
Luck/Fortune	Justice	Protection
Knowledge	Philanthropy	Inspiration
Benevolence	Exploration	Wisdom
Enthusiasm	Conviction	Hopefulness
Humor/Cheer	Success	Grace
Risk-taking	Extremism	Dogmatism
Grandosity	Excess	Fanaticism
Zealotry	Preachiness	Indulgence
Self-righteousness	Wastefulness	Intolerance

Before jumping into the specifics of how and where Jupiter shows up in your personal astrology, let's take a moment to do a worksheet to reflect on your innate connection with Jupiterian themes.

<u>**Here are some suggestions for using any of the worksheets in this book**</u>:

- There are no right or wrong answers to these prompts.
- Listen to your own inner voice and intuition.
- You may want to just put pen to paper and see what flows in a stream of consciousness.
- Or, you may want to sit with one question at a time, close your eyes, breathe, meditate on it, and listen and feel for answers arising in your thoughts, emotions and bodily sensations.
- Try not to overthink it. Don't consider what you "should" or "ought to" answer, or what other people might think. This book is a safe space for your private self-reflection to be honest about how you think and feel.
- Trust yourself to receive as valid and precious whatever information arises, without censorship or judgment.
- Remember that you can always revisit any of these worksheet prompts later and in as much depth as you want, so don't worry about this having to feel complete on your first pass.
- If you prefer to download .pdf versions of the worksheets to print out or work with as a digital

journal on your computer, here's how you
can do that.

Getting Seperate Worksheets

- Take the coupon code **MYJUPITER100**
- Go to www.robinwald.com, click on the Shop tab
- Add the item 'My Jupiter Worksheets' to your cart
  and go to check out
- Put your coupon code in the coupon field and
  the sheets will become free (you can download
  it two times!)

My Jupiter Keywords, Beliefs and Aspirations Worksheet

I believe I am here for a reason   Agree/Disagree

I aspire to align my life with a purpose   Agree/Disagree

I aspire to grow into my potential   Agree/Disagree

I have visions and dreams for my future   Agree/Disagree

I seek out guiding principles and truths   Agree/Disagree

I have inner faith, trust and optimism   Agree/Disagree

I yearn for spiritual connection   Agree/Disagree

I feel idealistic and optimistic about

I have faith in

I aspire to expand, learn, and grow around

I feel connected to a higher sense of Self/Source/Soul/God/ Mystery when

I have an abundance of

Some ways I feel I am especially blessed, prosperous and lucky are

I seek wisdom around

I am inspired to explore and have new experiences around

I feel happiest and most joyful when

I feel like I have grown and learned most from

I am most generous with

I am open-minded about

I can be close-minded, preachy or fanatical about

The most awesome experience or adventure I've had or
dream of having someday is

An area of my life where I tend to overdo it or go to extremes is

I have deep spiritual, religious and/or moral conviction around

<u>Jupiter Archetypes</u>

"Archetypes are universal, inborn models of people, behaviors, or personalities that play a role in influencing human behavior. They were introduced by the Swiss psychiatrist Carl Jung, who suggested that these archetypes were archaic forms of innate human knowledge passed down from our ancestors." -- American Psychological Association

According to Carl Jung archetypes are characteristics and traits of personality and behavior that originate in primordial images and symbols. Archetypes are universal patterns and themes within the collective consciousness to which we are all connected on an individual level. They are timeless and pervasive in art, poetry, music, dream images, stories, and memory. For instance, we all easily recognize the archetype of "mother" or "teacher" or "hero/heroine" and interact with these archetypes within our own sense of self and in our relationships with others.

Astrology is archetypal in its essence. Astrology offers the individual a personalized map and toolkit for deciphering the archetypal patterns they are most naturally attuned with and inclined towards.

According to archetypal astrologer, Richard Tarnas, "The basic principle of astrology is that the planets have a fundamental, cosmically based connection to specific archetypal forces or principles which influence human existence, and that the patterns formed by the planets in the heavens bear a meaningful correspondence to the patterns of human affairs on the Earth. In terms of individuals, the positions of the planets at the time and place of a person's birth are regarded as corresponding to the basic archetypal patterns of that person's life and character." *An Introduction to Archetypal Astrology* p. 1.

A way to understand your Sun sign is that you were born with a very strong attunement to that sign's archetypal pattern. For instance, if your Sun is in Leo, your core sense of self will feel strongly identified with many archetypal Leo traits and qualities, such as courage, leadership, creativity, vitality, generosity, heroism, and playfulness. Further, the placement of every single planet in the Universe at the exact time of your birth tells a symbolic and archetypal story about your unique qualities, traits, personality, purpose, and potential.

Archetypes operate in us and through us at varying levels of consciousness. The more conscious expression is often referred to as the "positive" "light" or "higher vibration," whereas less conscious awareness or uncon-scious expression of archetypal energies is referred to as the "negative" "shadow" "dark" or "lower vibration." Another way I like to understand this, in the Buddhist language of Thich Nhat Hanh, is as levels of skillfulness or relative unskillfulness. The good news is that we always have an ability to cultivate greater skillfulness, to raise our vibration, and to bring our shadow into light.

As an example, some key Jupiterian archetypes include the visionary, truth-seeker, guru, sage, teacher, and mentor. When a person embodies these archetypes in their light or higher vibration, that person is in search of wisdom, learning from and teaching others in a way that generously supports others' growth. There may be humility, awe, patience, grace, and joy in this higher Jupiterian expression. But when a person embodies this archetype in its shadow, there may be an excess of moral superiority, philosophical intolerance of others' viewpoints, or inflated ego. In its higher expression, the teacher meets students where they are and inspires their personal learning and perspective. In its shadow, the guru is overly dogmatic, forcing their own "truths" onto others in a rigid or righteous manner.

According to Tarnas, "All archetypes are Janus-faced, with positive and negative sides...The birth chart does not determine the moral vector of personal character. Nor does it determine ultimate "success" or "failure." It portrays rather the basic nature of the archetypal dynamics that inform that individual's life and character. How the individual copes with and grows through those particular dynamics, how she or he creatively embodies and integrates the diverse potentials of the birth chart, depends in the last analysis on the individual. The same archetype can express itself benignly or destructively, in an exalted way or an ignoble way, and to a great extent which of these occurs will be affected by the kind of consciousness that is brought to the situation." *An Introduction to Archetypal Astrology* p. 17

Astrology speaks to potential, not destiny. We can create conscious awareness around both our natural inclinations, as well as our choice to learn, practice and cultivate the highest vibration of the qualities we value. The better we understand and bring archetypal forces within us to consciousness, the more we become psychically integrated, healthy, and whole.

This book is specifically focused on helping you to

unpack and better understand the Jupiterian archetype and how it relates to your personal growth, life purpose, and potential.

My Jupiter Archetypes Worksheet

Wisdom Seeker	Shaman	Motivational Speaker
Guru	Sage	Mentor
Professor	Philosopher	Mystic
Teacher/Educator	Ethicist/Moralist	Prophet
Dreamer	World Traveler	Adventurer
Poet	Musician	Stoner/Substance User/Abuser
Visionary	Big-picture Thinker	Priestess/Priest/Rabbi/Preacher
Celebrity/Pop Star	Cultural Icon	Optimist
Media Personality	Influencer	Thrill-Seeker
Idealist	Fun-Lover	Explorer
Glutton	Extremist	Fanatic

From the list above, which archetypes do I connect with as strong aspects of my identity and personality, either in the past or present?

How have I expressed and shown up as these archetypes in my life? When? With who? In what settings?

How do I feel about myself when I embody and put forth this energy?

From the list above, are there any archetypes I aspire to develop more of in my personality and behavior? Which ones am I attracted to?

What might be different for me if I embodied and expressed more of that energy?

What action steps might I take to develop those archetypes within myself to bring that energy forth?

From the list above, are there any archetypes I feel negatively toward, triggered by, or have an aversion to? Which one(s)?

What feelings or sensations does that archetype trigger in my body? What thoughts am I telling myself about that archetype or people I know who strongly embody and express that quality?

In what ways do I sometimes embody and express that quality myself, consciously or unconsciously? What might I learn about myself and my values through honestly looking at this shadow expression of Jupiterian energy?

Jupiterian Quotes From Famous Jupiterian-Signature People

Dalai Lama -- Sun trine Jupiter, Pisces Midheaven
"I believe the very purpose of life is to seek happiness"

Oprah Winfrey -- Sagittarius Ascendant, Jupiter 6th house trine Midheaven
"Facing the truth really will set you free; Turn your wounds into wisdom."

"The biggest adventure you can take is to live the life of your dreams."

Tina Turner -- Sun in Sagittarius trine Jupiter in Pisces
"The future belongs to those who believe in the beauty of their own dreams."

"I'm not wise, but the beginning of wisdom is there; it's like a relaxing into – and an acceptance of – things."

"People think my life has been tough, but I think it's been a wonderful journey."

Walt Disney -- Sun and Mars conjunct in Sagittarius, Jupiter-Saturn Grand Conjunction in Capricorn, Pisces on 6th house cusp
"If you can dream it, you can do it."

"It's kind of fun to do the impossible."

Jim Morrison -- Sun in Sagittarius in 10th house highest placement in chart, Jupiter trine Mercury, sextile Venus
"If my poetry aims to achieve anything, it's to deliver people from the limited ways in which they see and feel."

Jimi Hendrix -- Sun/Venus/Mercury conjunction in Sagittarius, Jupiter conjunct Moon in Cancer
"Music is my religion."

"Imagination is the key to my lyrics. The rest is painted with a little science fiction."

Professor Dumbledore -- headmaster, wise sage, professor of Hogwarts in J.K. Rowling's *Harry Potter*
"It is my belief that the truth is generally preferable to lies."

"It matters not what someone is born, but what they grow to be."

Chapter 2: My Natal Jupiter

In this chapter, you will identify all of the things you can about Jupiter in your natal (birth) chart - it's sign, house, relationships (aspects) to other planets and points in your chart, and more. Your natal chart is completely unique to you and is a map of where every planet was in the zodiac at that moment of your birth. Only another baby born in the same location on the globe within 4 minutes of you would have the same chart. Astrology takes the perspective that taking your first breath in this world under a specific and unique configuration of planetary energies holds meaning for you, about your essential nature, gifts, and potential.

Since this book is about Jupiter, the first step is to identify everything you can about Jupiter in your chart, so that you have all the information you will need to interpret, understand, and create meaning for yourself in the chapters following. Specifically, in Chapter 3 you will dive deeper into understanding your Jupiter sign, in Chapter 4 you will explore your Jupiter house, in Chapter 5 you will explore your Jupiter relationships to other planets, and in Chapters 6 and 7 you will explore cycles of Jupiter transits through-out your life.

How to calculate your natal (birth) chart:

In order to calculate your birth chart, you will need to know your date and year of birth, the location of your birth (city/state/country) and the time of your birth. An exact birth time is really important, as this is what determines the rising sign and degrees on your Ascendant, as well as the signs on all of the house cusps, and the house placements of your planets.

If you don't have an exact birth time, here are some suggestions for trying to find it out:

- Check your birth certificate -- you can contact the state or local birth records department to request a copy if you don't already have it in your possession
- If you don't have your birth certificate, or if the time wasn't recorded on the birth certificate, check to see if the time was recorded in a baby book or birth announcement
- Ask a parent, older sibling or relative if they remember the exact time or the approximate hour, time of day, or other memories connected to your time of birth
- Contact the hospital or place you were born to see if they kept a record
- Work with a professional astrologer skilled in chart rectification to support you to arrive at a best guess of the time, based on your attributes and the timing of key impactful life experiences

If you are working without a known or exact birth time, you can still use this workbook!! Everything about Jupiter's sign, its aspects to your other planets, and its transit cycles will still be correct and give you incredibly valuable insights. What won't be accurate is the discussion of the houses (ie. where in your chart this is occurring). Using this workbook to reflect on your lived experiences might actually help you to "rectify" and arrive at what intuitively feels like an accurate birth time based on where you most experience Jupiter themes in your life. Your self-work in this book can provide valuable information you might choose to bring to a professional astrologer skilled in chart rectification.

Okay, so you have your birth date, place, and time info. What's the next step? There are several good ways to get an accurate calculation of your natal chart.

The most advanced and complicated way is to spend a few months learning complex math to hand-calculate the degree placement of your Ascendant, Midheaven and every planet, using a calculator, trigonometric equations, and an ephemeris. I don't recommend this method for a lay person. But if this idea and level of learning jazzes you up, I recommend the book *Simply Math: A Comprehensive Guide to Easy and Accurate Chart Calculation*, by Lauran Fowks and Lynn Sellon (included in Appendix A) to support you in that endeavor.

Another way is to engage a professional consulting astrologer to run your chart for you. There are many advantages to working with a professional astrologer to help you create awareness of yourself, especially if you are a novice or beginner in learning the symbols and language of astrology.

Through partnership and conversation, a good astrologer will evoke understanding around your natal chart's potential in the context of how you have actually used and interacted with your unique planetary configurations up to this point in your life. If you would like me to run your chart for you, or consult with me about your chart, please visit my website www.robinwald.com for options or to contact me.

If you are a more avid enthusiast or intermediate student, I recommend you invest in purchasing a trustworthy professional astrology software program for yourself that you can learn and grow with over time. I am personally very grateful for how much I've learned through playing with my professional Solar Fire software. This program has all of the bells and whistles an astrology professional or enthusiast could ever employ and more!

Luckily, the very easiest and free way to get an accurately calculated chart is to go online to one of many websites that offer free astrological chart calculation. The one I recommend is Astro.com (AstroDienst).

Astro.com Free Natal Chart Calculation
https://www.astro.com

From the main page on Astro.com, select "Charts and Calculations" -- this will bring you to a page entitled "Free Charts, Calculations and Data." From there, select "Chart Drawing/Ascendant." On the Birth Data Entry page, type in your birth info (date, location, and time of birth). I suggest saving and printing out a copy of your chart and data, so that you have it readily available to work with as you make your way through the chapters and exercises in this book.

A clarifying note about choosing house systems when

running a natal chart. Everything I offer in this book is rooted in Western astrological traditions, not in Vedic, Chinese or other systems in which I claim no expertise. Please reach out to a professional or other books and resources if that is your area of interest. I use the Placidus house system in calculating and interpreting charts for my clients. For a variety of historical reasons, this has become the most common house system used in modern astrology, though not the only one. If you are working with whole sign houses, porphyry or any other house division system, the guidance in this book still applies, and you will interpret and find meaning by reflecting on your own experiences based on that house placement system. If you are a more advanced student or practitioner, it might be an interesting exercise to run your chart via different house systems and see how that changes your placement and understanding of Jupiter in your chart and life.

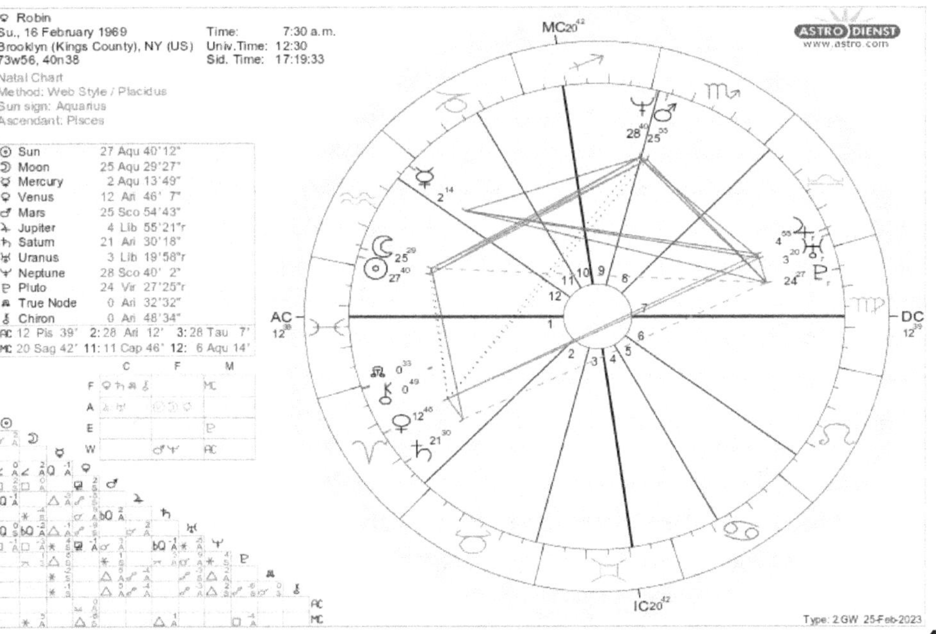

On the previous page is an example of my birth chart, calculated on Astro.com

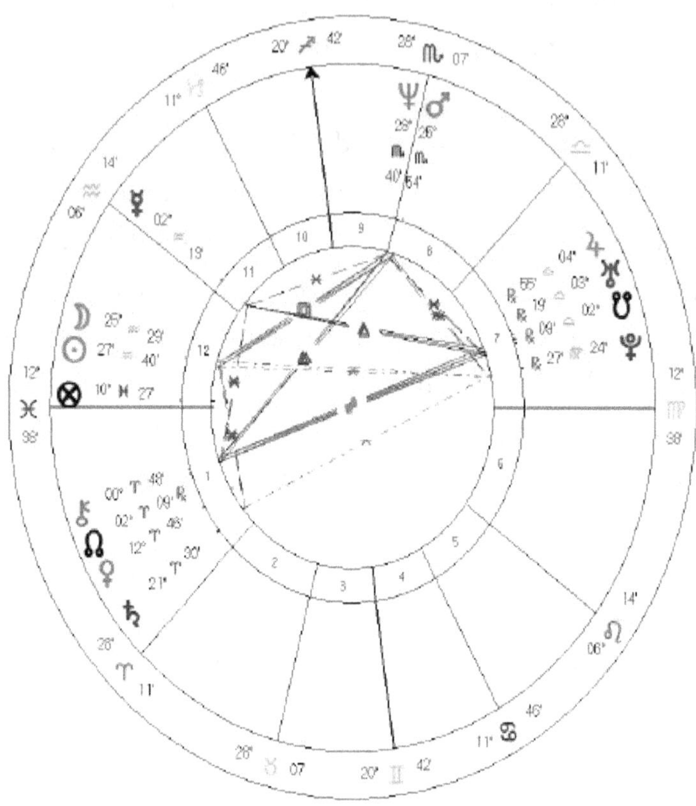

Above is an example of my birth chart wheel using Solar Fire professional astrology software (wheel only)

Let's do a walk-through of my sample birth charts as created in Astro.com and in Solar Fire, to identify key elements related to Jupiter in my chart, so that you will understand what to look for in your own chart. Note that the visual wheel designs differ from Astro.com and Solar Fire, but all the information you need is still there. Astro.com marks the Ascendant with AC and the Midheaven with MC. In Solar Fire, the Ascendant is the dark-lined cusp between

House 12 and 1, and there is an arrow point on the cusp between the 9th and 10th houses at the Midheaven.

If you have more advanced astrology knowledge and

Reference Table of Astrological Symbols		
Planets	**Signs**	**Aspects**
☉ Sun	♈ Aries	☌ Conjunction
☽ Moon	♉ Taurus	✷ Sextile
☿ Mercury	♊ Gemini	☐ Square
♀ Venus	♋ Cancer	△ Trine
♂ Mars	♌ Leo	⚻ Quincunx
♃ Jupiter	♍ Virgo	☍ Opposition
♄ Saturn	♎ Libra	
♅ Uranus	♏ Scorpio	℞ Retrograde
♆ Neptune	♐ Sagittarius	
♇ Pluto	♑ Capricorn	
⚷ Chiron	♒ Aquarius	
AC Ascendant	♓ Pisces	
MC Midheaven		
☋ South Node		
☊ North Node		

don't need this guidance in reading your chart, feel free to jump ahead to the worksheets in this chapter.

Jupiter's sign, degrees and house

- Using both charts as a reference, see if you can find Jupiter ♃
- Do you see that my natal Jupiter is at 04° ♎ 55' (four degrees and fifty-five minutes of Libra)?
- Do you see that it is in the 7th house?
- Do you see the Rx next to it, showing that Jupiter was Retrograde at the time of my birth?

Jupiter's aspects to other planets

Chapter 5 will provide much more guidance to help you with this complex and important subject. For now, we are just trying to locate and identify.

Do you see that Jupiter ♃ is right next to (conjunct) Uranus ♅ which is one degree away at 3 degrees of Libra?

My Jupiter is also conjunct my South Node ☋ at 2 degrees of Libra and in opposition (180 degrees directly across, indicated by a line with this symbol ☍) to my North Node ☊ in 2 degrees of Aries ♈ in my 1st house? (Note that Astro. com default settings for beginner chart calculation does not show the South Node but it would be located exactly 180 degrees opposite the North Node).

Do you see that Jupiter is sextile Mercury ☿ at 2 degrees of Aquarius ♒ in the 11th house (approximately 120 degrees away, indicated by a triangle △)?

Do you see that Jupiter is opposing Chiron ⚷ at 0 degrees of Aries in my 1st house? (approximately 180 degrees away ☍)

Do you see that in the Astro.com chart, which works with a wider aspect orb (again, more on understanding aspects and orbs in chapter 5), it shows Jupiter opposing my Venus ♀ at 12 degrees of Aries in the 1st house? But on the Solar Fire chart, where I use a 6-degree orb for planets other than the Sun and Moon, it does not show those planets in opposition?

Do you see that my Sun ☉ and my Moon ☽ are both in Aquarius ♒ 12th house, not in either of the Jupiter-ruled signs of Sagittarius ♐ or Pisces ♓?

Do you see that the sign on my Ascendant (AC, the line between the 12th and 1st house, also called the Rising Sign) is in the Jupiter-ruled sign of Pisces ♓?

Do you see that the sign on my Midheaven (MC, the arrow at the very top of the chart dividing the 9th and 10th houses) is in the Jupiter-ruled sign of Sagittarius ♐?

I've included my completed worksheet sample in Appendix D for reference.

Your turn!

The My Natal Jupiter Worksheet on the following page is where you can record all the important data about Jupiter in your natal chart. You may want to bookmark, dog-ear, or copy this page, as you will keep referring back to it for key information you need to access for later chapters and worksheet exercises.

My Natal Jupiter Worksheet

My natal Jupiter is in the sign of

____

My natal Jupiter's degree and minutes is

____

My natal Jupiter is in the ___________ house
(accurate house placement is dependent on having an
accurate birth time)

My natal Jupiter is Direct/ Retrograde (circle which applies)

My natal Jupiter is connected to these planets/points by
aspect

   Planet/Point   Aspect

____________________   ____________________

____________________   ____________________

____________________   ____________________

____________________   ____________________

____________________   ____________________

Is my natal Jupiter part of a special aspect pattern (stellium, grand trine, T-square, grand cross, or yod? (see appendix B for more on this)

How Jupiterian Am I? Worksheet

Referring to your natal chart, let's see how strong your Jupiter signature is. This worksheet will ask you to look for planets and placements you have in Sagittarius or Pisces, the two signs "ruled" by Jupiter and associated with strong Jupiterian energy.

1. Jupiter in Sagittarius or Pisces — Yes/No

2. Sun in Sagittarius or Pisces — Yes/No

3. Moon in Sagittarius or Pisces — Yes/No

4. Ascendant (AC 12th/1st house cusp) in Sagittarius or Pisces — Yes/No

5. Midheaven (MC 9th/10th house cusp) in Sagittarius or Pisces — Yes/No

6. Three or more planets/AC/MC in Sagittarius or Pisces — Yes/No

7. Jupiter in aspect to the Sun, Moon, AC or MC — Yes/No

8. Jupiter in the 1st house — Yes/No

9. Sun, Moon or concentration of planets in the 9th or 12th house — Yes/No

10. Jupiter is part of a Stellium, Grand Trine, T-square, Grand Cross, Yod — Yes/No

11. Day Chart (Sun in 7-12 house) — Yes/No

12. Jupiter is retrograde — Yes/No

Extra worksheet space

Chapter 3: My Jupiter by Sign

Reference Guide to The Signs

In this section, I offer you a reference guide to the central themes and keywords for the different zodiac signs, and some ways that Jupiter may express itself in each sign. This is a foundational abbreviated guide, not a fully exhaustive list of every possible way to understand each sign or how Jupiter shows up in that sign. What's most important is your own insight and self-awareness as you work with this information.

The twelve zodiac signs are formed by a combination of four elemental qualities of fire, earth, air, and water that each operate in three modal qualities of cardinal, fixed, or mutable, resulting in twelve distinct and unique expressions.

Triplicities are groups of signs in the same element

Fire Signs -- Aries, Leo, Sagittarius
The energy of fire is creative, inspired, passionate and confident.

Earth Signs -- Taurus, Virgo, Capricorn
The energy of earth is grounded, practical, stable and dependable.

Air Signs -- Gemini, Libra, Aquarius
The energy of air is intellectual, social, quick-witted, and idea-oriented.

Water Signs -- Cancer, Scorpio, Pisces
The energy of water is emotional, sensitive, empathic and intuitive.

Quadruplicities are groups of signs that share the same modal quality

Cardinal Signs -- Aries, Cancer, Libra, Capricorn
Cardinal is the quality of initiating and beginning, and is associated with the solstices and equinoxes, kicking off the new seasons of Spring, Summer, Fall, and Winter.

Fixed Signs -- Taurus, Leo, Scorpio, Aquarius
Fixed is the quality of persisting, persevering, stubbornness, and resisting change.

Mutable Signs -- Gemini, Virgo, Sagittarius, Pisces
Mutable is the quality of adapting, changing, letting go, and moving on.

Jupiter will express itself very differently in a cardinal fire sign (Aries) versus a fixed earth sign (Taurus) versus a mutable air sign (Gemini). The guide below will help you make sense of each sign and Jupiter's placement there.

Obviously, Jupiter only occupies one of the twelve signs at the time of your birth, as reflected in your natal chart, so you will want to read the section on your Jupiter sign first. Beyond that, you might read the rest of this reference guide to expand your general understanding of the characteristics of the other signs, especially if you are newer to astrology. You can also use this guide to look up and read about a loved one's Jupiter placement in a different sign than yours. This guide will also be helpful for understanding key energies as Jupiter moves through the different signs each year of your life by transit (which we will look at more in Chapter 7).

You will notice that some of the keywords, archetypes and symbols resonate with you as positive and desirable, while others may feel negative or undesirable. As discussed in Chapter 1, archetypal energies present along a spectrum from conscious to unconscious, skillful to unskillful, high to low vibration, awake or in shadow. At different points in your life's journey, you may have experienced different aspects of this energy, as part of your soul's growth experience at that time. Sometimes you may embody and use this energy skillfully, and at other times you may be less skillful and struggle.

<u>The sign Jupiter was in at your birth informs the central themes around which you are inclined to:</u>

- grow, expand and learn
- feel optimistic, inspired, visionary, purposeful or adventurous
- feel especially faithful, blessed, fortunate or prosperous
- operate on a BIG scale
- have ideals, beliefs and moral convictions
- take things to excess or extremes

Aries ♈

Mode and Element: Cardinal Fire
Ruling Planet: Mars

Keywords: initiative, action, passion, courage, willpower, independence, autonomy, athleticism, competitiveness, risk-taking, assertiveness, bravery, boldness, self-confidence, impulsivity, drive, aggression, self-centeredness, egoism

Archetypes and Symbols: ruler, king, emperor, Mars, boss, solopreneur, warrior, military/combat person, martial artist, hero, competitive athlete, fire, ram, weapons, Tarot: suit of wands, the Emperor, the Tower

Associated health issues: accidents, injury, surgery, burns, inflammation, ulcers, headaches, brain issues, impulsivity, explosive temper/rage

Jupiter in Aries potential expressions

- seeks to grow through self-assertion, action and initiative
- feeling optimistic or purposeful around self-directed goals
- a natural inner faith in oneself, high self-esteem and self-confidence
- big vitality and energy, a desire to be physically active and competitive
- ideals around independence, boldness to take risks and winning at goals
- overly arrogant or aggressive, excessively risk-taking

♈

Taurus ♉

Mode and Element: Fixed Earth
Ruling Planet: Venus

<u>*Keywords*</u>: beauty, sensuality, security, stability, comfort, material resources, money/possessions, fertility, productivity, groundedness, conscientiousness, integrity, values, self-worth, physical body, materialism, abundance/scarcity, rigidity, caution, stubbornness, aversion to change

<u>*Archetypes and Symbols*</u>: Mother Earth, goddess, Venus/Aphrodite, cow/bull, coins/money, stockbroker/banker, gardener, chef, foodie, makeup/hair/fashion, artist, designer, model, Tarot: suit of pentacles, the Empress, the Hierophant

<u>*Associated health issues*</u>: throat issues, cold sores, weight issues, eating disorders, constipation, hoarding

Jupiter in Taurus potential expressions

- seeks to grow through physical experiences, productivity, reliability
- feeling optimistic or purposeful around one's skills and physical resources
- natural inner faith in one's own beauty, value, and resourcefulness
- big need for security, groundedness, physical comfort, connection to nature
- ideals around nature, beauty, sensuality and pleasure
- overly cautious, risk-averse, frugal, materialistic, stubborn

♉

Gemini ♊
Mode and Element: Mutable Air
Ruling Planet: Mercury

Keywords: communication, wit, speaking, listening, reading, writing, media, advertising, learning, teaching, thinking, social interactions, friendliness, humor, exchange of ideas, curiosity, talkativeness, versatility, indecision, duality/opposites, adaptability, agility, movement, short-distance travel, non-binary spectrum

Archetypes and Symbols: messenger, communicator, trickster, joker, writer, speaker, teacher, storyteller, social media personality, advertising professional, "Jack of all trades master of none", gift of gab, comedian/jester, ADHD, youngster, worry-wart, speech and language specialist, linguist, musician, twins, Mercury/Hermes, bi/pan-sexual, Tarot: suit of swords, the Lovers, the Magician

Associated health issues: worry, anxiety, attention deficit, hyperactivity, nervous system disorders, tics, insomnia, lung/respiratory issues

Jupiter in Gemini potential expressions
- seeks to grow through learning, speaking, and socializing
- feeling optimistic or purposeful around ideas and learning
- a natural inner faith in one's intelligence, intellectual curiosity and ability to communicate with others
- big ideas and aptitude for taking in information,

    multi-tasking, jumping from one project to another, pursuing a wide range of interests
- ideals around music, language, mental capabilities, learning, friends
- overly talkative, restless, hyperactive in body and mind, indecisive, excessive overthinking, anxiety, ADHD

♊

Cancer ♋
Mode and Element: Cardinal Water
Ruling Planet: Moon

<u>Keywords</u>: parenting, family, children, ancestors, home, caretaking, nurturing, compassion, empathy, protectiveness, emotionality, sensitivity, moodiness, intuition, nostalgia, self-protection, sentimentality

<u>Archetypes and Symbols</u>: mother, parent, nurturer, caretaker, nurse, homemaker, homebody, realtor, childcare worker, eldercare worker, cry-baby, crabs and other sea/land creatures, phases and cycles, the Moon, Tarot: suit of water, the Moon, the Chariot

<u>Associated health issues</u>: sadness, depression, loneliness, overeating, weight and fluid retention, stomach and breast issues

<u>Jupiter in Cancer potential expressions</u>
- seeks to grow through caretaking others and developing love and sensitivity

- feeling optimistic or purposeful around family, home, and domestic life
- a natural inner faith in one's feelings, intuition, parenting ability
- big desire to nurture and protect others
- ideals around parenthood, children, family
- overly emotional, sentimental, self-protective, private, nostalgic

Leo ♌

Mode and Element: Fixed Fire
Ruling Planet: Sun

Keywords: creativity, confidence, self-expression, boldness, charisma, leadership, dignity, playfulness, warmth, generosity, big-heartedness, flirtiness, sex-appeal, drama/theatrics, nobility, heroism, self-assuredness, courage, loyalty, pride, vanity, need for recognition, center of attention, self-aggrandizement, egoism, narcissism

Archetypes and Symbols: noble, king, leader, celebrity, actor, entertainer, hero, protector, savior, CEO, artist, creative, child, player, narcissist, lions, the sun, thrones, victory, Tarot: suit of wands, Strength, the Sun

Associated health issues: heart/valve/artery conditions, high blood pressure, palpitations, intense emotions, burnout

Jupiter in Leo potential expressions

- seeks to grow through creativity and generous leadership
- feeling optimistic or purposeful around creativity and self-expression
- a natural inner faith in one's own vitality and in life itself
- big sense of courage, pride and leadership ability
- ideals around joy, flair, creativity, art, fun, life as a drama
- overly prideful or arrogant, excessive need for attention and recognition, god-complex

♌

Virgo ♍

Mode and Element: Mutable Earth
Ruling Planet: Mercury

Keywords: attention to details, critical analysis, discernment, keenness of mind, precision, service, thoughtfulness, management of self and others, helpfulness, planning, orderliness, skill, perfectionism, conscientiousness, criticism, control, all-or-nothing thinking, judgment, health, routines

Archetypes and Symbols: manager, organizer, executive, planner, data analyst, editor, nit-picker, control-freak, martyr, craftsperson, mechanic, physician, diagnostician, hands-on healer, health and fitness instructor, nutritionist, cook, housekeeper, servant, virgin, home and hearth, harvest, Tarot: suit of pentacles, the Hermit

Associated health issues: overeating, obesity, stomach ailments, ulcers, irritable bowel syndrome, obsessive-compulsive disorder, insomnia

Jupiter in Virgo potential expressions
- seeks to grow through helpfulness, hard work, and self-discipline
- feeling optimistic or purposeful around being of service through one's analytical, organizational and management abilities
- a natural inner faith in one's own discernment between right and wrong
- big sense of precision and attention to detail
- ideals around perfection and martyrdom
- overly critical with self and others, rigid, micro-managing, judgemental

♍

Libra ♎
Mode and Element: Cardinal Air
Ruling Planet: Venus

Keywords: interpersonal relationship, partnership, cooperation, sociability, harmony, balance, objectivity, fair-mindedness, justice, equity, diplomacy, principles, likability, indecision, accommodation, compromise, peacefulness, vanity, need to be liked, people-pleasing

Archetypes and Symbols: friend, lover, judge, advisor, counselor, mediator, lawyer, giver, peacekeeper, diplomat, Athena, Lady Justice, people-pleaser, owls, scales, balances, blind justice, Tarot: suit of swords, Justice

<u>Associated health issues</u>: adrenal fatigue, stress, indecision, dryness, skin issues, kidney and adrenal disorders, bladder problems

<u>Jupiter in Libra potential expressions</u>:

- seeks to grow through interpersonal relationship
- feeling optimistic or purposeful about harmonious relationships and cooperation
- a natural inner faith in one's fair-mindedness and balanced objectivity
- big sense of inter-relatedness, interpersonal connection, prioritizing others and relationships above oneself
- ideals around beauty, peace, harmony, equity, justice
- overly accommodating of others, excessive thinking or indecisiveness, overly concerned with outer aesthetics/ vanity, big need to be liked

<u>Scorpio</u> ♏

Mode and Element: Fixed Water
Ruling Planet: Pluto, Mars (traditional)

<u>Keywords</u>: intensity, depth, desire, power, transformation, resilience, rebirth, sexuality, control over self and others, invulnerability, privacy, secrecy, guardedness, stoicism, mystery, magic, occult, darkness, manipulation, suspicion, loyalty

<u>Archetypes and Symbols</u>: stoic, researcher, psychiatrist/ psychologist, transformer, detective, investigator, security guard, boss, power broker, abuser/abused, covert operative, criminologist, mental health professional, trauma therapist, witch/wizard/occultist, dominatrix, the under-world, death and resurrection, Pluto/Hades, Persephone, phoenix, snake, scorpion, eagle, Tarot: suit of water, Death

Associated health issues: sexual problems, ovarian/testes issues, reproductive issues, infertility, colorectal issues, sex hormone imbalances, menstrual problems, depression, mental health disorders

Jupiter in Scorpio potential expressions
- seeks to grow and transform through intense, challenging or crisis experiences
- feeling optimistic or purposeful about research and probing into the depth of matters
- a natural inner faith in one's own self-mastery and self-protection around emotional vulnerability or powerlessness
- big sense of intensity, depth, inner emotional and psychological processing
- ideals around magic, mysticism, human psychology, sexuality and deep understanding beyond the superficial
- overly secretive, suspicious, manipulative or unforgiving, excessively guarded, control-freak, inflated libido or sexual addiction

♏

Sagittarius ♐

Mode and Element: Mutable Fire
Ruling Planet: Jupiter

Jupiter is the planetary ruler of Sagittarius, so the keywords, attributes and symbols discussed in Chapter 1 relate to Sagittarian Jupiter. Being born with Jupiter in its sign of rulership gives you a very strong Jupiterian attunement and personality.

Keywords: expansion, growth, purpose, optimism, joviality, idealism, spirituality, wisdom, prophecy, faithfulness, abundance, aspiration, adventure, connection to higher meaning, possibility, potential, righteousness, justice, fanaticism, dogmatism, extremism

Archetypes and Symbols: wisdom/truth-seeker, sage, teacher, guru, philosopher, explorer/adventurer, optimist, visionary/dreamer, motivational speaker, celebrity, larger-than-life icon, mystic/prophet, moralist/ethicist, preacher, media personality, bows and arrows, rainbows, archers, thunderbolts, heavens, sky, eagles, centaurs, horses, Tarot: suit of wands, Temperance, Wheel of Fortune

Associated health issues: hip/thigh/leg issues, sciatica, back pain, spinal issues

Jupiter in Sagittarius potential expressions:
- seeks to grow through faith, spirituality, broad learning opportunities, travel
- feeling optimistic or motivated about learning, teaching,

ideals and aspirations
- a natural inner faith in life's blessings, good fortune and abundance
- big sense of adventure, wanderlust and growing through new experiences
- ideals around soul potential and connecting with a higher purpose
- overly dogmatic, idealistic, inattentive to the here and now, preachy, on a soapbox about one's truth being the Truth

♐

Capricorn ♑
Mode and Element: Cardinal Earth
Ruling Planet: Saturn

Keywords: hard work, discipline, persistence, endurance, ambition, accomplishment, mastery, authority, responsibility, productivity, adulthood, tradition, patience, planning, structure, status, success, fear, scarcity, seriousness, stodginess, perseverance, commitment, legacy, honor, integrity, enslavement, burden

Archetypes and Symbols: adult, patriarch, father, boss, CEO, corporate executive, workaholic, political leader, government official, authority figure, historian, public figure, ancestor, rule-maker, rule-follower/enforcer, disciplinarian, Father Time, old man winter, Saturn, conservative, traditionalist, builder, earth-mover, goats, Tarot: suit of pentacles, the Devil, the World

Associated health issues: bone and joint issues, knee pain, muscular pain, chronic pain, chronic fatigue syndrome, stiffness

Jupiter in Capricorn potential expressions

- seeks to grow through discipline, commitment and patient effort
- feeling optimistic or purposeful about proving oneself and earning recognition, rank and status for one's accomplishments
- a natural inner faith in one's work ethic and mastery
- big sense of responsibility, authority, tradition, discipline
- ideals around integrity, honor, societal rules and paradigms
- overly serious, fearful, workaholic, bound up with "shoulds and have tos", slow to change, conformist to socially accepted norms

♑

Aquarius ♒

Mode and Element: Fixed Air
Ruling Planet: Uranus, Saturn (traditional)

Keywords: uniqueness, individuality, unconventionality, intelligence, freedom, insight, authenticity, humanitarianism, eccentricity, non-conformity, wit, detachment, rebelliousness, inventiveness, innovation, futuristic, out-of-the-box, idealism, progress, coldness, other-worldly, alien

<u>**Archetypes and Symbols**</u>: innovator, inventor, hippie, rebel, teenager, LGBTQ+, free-spirit, anarchist, outsider, alien, change-maker, futurist, engineer, techno-geek, physicist, community activist, humanitarian, water-bearer, uranium, technology, lightning flashes, stars/constellations/galaxies, Tarot: suit of swords, the Star

<u>**Associated health issues:**</u> circulation issues, ankle issues, nervous system issues, overthinking, rumination, insomnia

Jupiter in Aquarius potential expressions

- seeks to grow through authentic free expression of one's own truth and originality
- feeling optimistic or purposeful about knowledge, open-mindedness, and innovative ideas
- a natural inner faith and pride in one's own uniqueness, intellectual capabilities, non-conformity
- big sense of humanitarianism and concern for the dignity and freedom of all beings
- ideals around social justice, progress, and rejection of conventional authoritarian paradigms
- emotionally detached, over-thinking, excessively rebellious, rule-breaking, eccentric, socially awkward

♒

Pisces ♓

Mode and Element: Mutable Water
Ruling Planet: Neptune, Jupiter (traditional)

Jupiter is the traditional planetary ruler of Pisces, so many of the Jupiter keywords, attributes and archetypes discussed in chapter 1 relate to Pisces. Being born with Jupiter in its sign of rulership gives you a very strong Jupiterian attunement and personality.

Keywords: sensitivity, intuition, perception, compassion, soulfulness, vision, imagination, creativity, transcendence, selflessness, altruism, spirituality, mysticism, devotion, escapism, addiction, victimhood, go with the flow, union, merging, lacking boundaries, co-dependence, sacrifice, forgiveness, surrender, faith

Archetypes and Symbols: musician, poet, bleeding-heart, volunteer, philanthropist, healer, giver, empath, channel, psychic, dreamer, visionary, introvert, addict, yogi, meditator, guru, surfer, spiritualist, escapist, gamer, loner, crybaby, bodhisattva, hospital worker, hospice worker, Neptune, trident, oceans, clouds, fish and water creatures, dream images, Tarot: suit of cups, Hanged Man, the Moon

Associated health issues: foot and toe problems, swelling and edema, immune and auto-immune problems, circulatory problems, addiction and substance abuse, sadness, broken-heartedness

Jupiter in Pisces potential expressions

- seeks to grow through transcendent experiences, connection to spiritual ideals and beliefs, imagination, music/art/film/poetry, spiritual practices
- feeling optimistic or purposeful about surrendering to grace, being in the flow, connecting on a soul level, merging with the Infinite/Oneness
- a natural inner faith in one's emotional sensitivity, empathy and intuition
- big sense of empathy, soulfulness, yearning to alleviate suffering of self and others
- ideals around transcendence, merging with others and Source, lovingkindness
- overly escapist, avoidant or procrastinating around "ordinary" life tasks, overly identified with victimization and suffering, substance abuse or dependency

♓

My Jupiter Sign Reflection Worksheet

My Jupiter is in the sign of _________________________________

Some of the keywords for my natal Jupiter's sign are (from Reference Guide to the Signs in the previous pages of this chapter):

Some of the archetypes and symbols of my natal Jupiter's sign are (from Reference Guide to the Signs in the previous pages of this chapter):

Which of these keywords, archetypes and symbols do I relate to strongly? How do they show up as "big" themes in my life?

How have I grown and improved myself through lessons
learned around these themes?

What are my aspirations and ideals around these themes?

When and how have I experienced good fortune, abundance,
or generosity around these themes?

When and how have I experienced some of the excesses or extremes of Jupiter in this sign?

Future Visioning around my Jupiter's natal sign

Do I have a specific dream or vision for my future that aligns with my Jupiter sign?
Describe this vision in as much detail as possible. What do I see? Where am I? Who is with me? How do I feel? What am I thinking? What am I doing? How did I get to this place where I've actualized my dream into reality?

What action steps might I take to move forward towards achieving my vision?

What might interfere with me taking those next steps?

What inner and outer resources might I rely on to help me overcome potential obstacles?

<u>Jupiter Retrograde Reflection</u> (complete if Jupiter is retrograde in your chart)

How does my Jupiter energy express more as an inner versus an outer expansiveness? Am I highly introspective about my spiritual beliefs, ideals, and aspirations? Have I felt hesitant, delayed, resistant, or unlucky around my personal growth and living into my soul purpose?

Extra worksheet space

Chapter 4: My Jupiter by House

Your birth chart (and every horoscope chart) is divided into twelve parts called houses. Each house represents a different part of your life experience. Here is a helpful summary of the meanings associated with each house.

Reference Guide to The Houses

1st house

self, identity, personality, physical appearance, how we present to others, our outer expression or role we play, lifestyle, personal expression, vitality, personal will and desire

2nd house

resources, personal skills and abilities, self-worth, values, money, assets/debt, possessions, security, livelihood

3rd house

written and oral communication, language, intellect, siblings, neighbors, learning, curiosity, socialization, short distance journeys

4th house

home, family, parents, childhood, roots, ancestors, parenting, privacy, sanctuary, real estate

5th house

confidence, self-expression, creativity, leadership, heroism, nobility, play, pleasure, amusement, children, romance, risk-taking, love/sex affairs

6th house

daily routines, health/sickness, fitness, nutrition, hygiene, work/jobs, service, servitude, colleagues/employees, small animals/pets

7th house

one-on-one relationships, intimate partners, spouses, cooperation, business partners, counseling, coaching, advocacy, legal contracts and lawsuits, enemies

8th house

power, transformation, crisis, sex, death, rebirth, mental health, psychology, other people's money and resources, inheritance, shared property, marriage, psychic/occult, magic

9th house

higher education, philosophy, religion, ethics, global travel, culture, broadening horizons, truth, adventure, legal affairs, divine law

10th house

professional career, vocation, public role, reputation, honor, accomplishment, social status, bosses, authority figures

11th house

groups of friends, social groups, community, tribe, collective, teenagers, humanity, shared ideals

12th house

Soul, inner world, subconscious, unconscious, shadow, past lives and karma, introversion, sacrifice, memory, dreams, secrets, transcendence, hidden enemies, compassion, victimization, hospitals, prisons

"Whatever house Jupiter is in, it is there that one can most immediately experience faith, trust, and hope for the future. In this field of experience one can most easily develop an optimistic awareness of one's capacity for growth and self-improvement."
-- Stephen Arroyo, Chart Interpretation Handbook, p. 126

<u>The house where Jupiter resides in your chart is the area of your life where you</u>:

- aim to grow, expand and learn
- feel optimistic, inspired, visionary, purposeful or adventurous
- feel especially faithful, blessed, fortunate and/ or prosperous
- operate on a BIG scale
- have ideals, beliefs and moral convictions
- take things to excess or extremes

My Jupiter House Reflection Worksheet

My Jupiter is in the ________________ house

Some main themes of my Jupiter house are (from Reference Guide to the Houses in the previous pages of this chapter):

In what ways do I feel "faith, trust and hope for the future" in this area of my life?

How have I strived to grow and improve myself in this area of my life?

Do I feel a strong sense of soul purpose, meaning, or conviction around the themes of this house?

How and when have I felt lucky, blessed, abundant or generous around these themes?

In what ways am I prone to excess in this area of my life?

Future Visioning around my Jupiter's natal house

Do I have a specific dream or vision for my future that aligns with my Jupiter house? Describe this vision in as much detail as possible. What do I see? Where am I? Who is with me? How do I feel? What am I thinking? What am I doing? How did I get to this place where I've actualized my dream into reality?

What action steps might I take to move forward towards achieving my vision?

What might interfere with me taking those next steps?

What inner and outer resources might I rely on to help me overcome potential obstacles?

Chapter 5: My Jupiter Aspects

Based on where planets are in the cosmos and zodiac at the time of your birth, geometrical connections are formed between some planets and points in your chart. These connections are called "aspects" and add a deeper layer and dimension to the story of who you are and have the potential to become.

There are 360 degrees in a circle and in the zodiac, with each of the twelve signs taking up 30 degrees, and each degree having sixty minutes. Each astrological sign begins at zero degrees and zero minutes (0°00') and ends at twenty-nine degrees and fifty-nine minutes (29°59'). When planets are a certain number of degrees apart, their geometric relationship influences each other in specific ways.

If I already lost you with the geometry and math -- don't worry! An online chart calculation tool like the one on Astro.com will do the math and display the aspect relationships right on your natal chart diagram, using colored lines and symbols to make it easy for you to see what planets are relating to each other. You already began to identify these aspects when you did the My Natal Jupiter Worksheet in Chapter 2. In this chapter, you will explore what these aspects mean for you.

Just like in human relationships, the relationships between planetary archetypes in your chart can be complicated. Sometimes planets support each other and play well together; sometimes they create friction, discord, or feel forced. Some relationships add a lot of value to your life and influence you in profound ways. Some relationships feel so natural and easy that you might take them for granted or not see them for their full potential. Some relationships have an element of strain and tension, which may frustrate you, or motivate you constructively to make necessary changes in yourself or your circumstances. Like I said, it's complicated.

Here is a list of the major aspects you may find between your natal Jupiter and other planets:

Aspect	Deg.	Symbol	Color	Interpretation of the Energy
Conjunct	0 °	☌	Black	Amplifying, merging, concentrating, blending
Sextile	60 °	✳	Blue	Friendly, helpful, lucky
Trine	120 °	△	Blue	Cooperative, harmonious, integrated balanced, flowing, natural, easy
Square	90 °	□	Red	Challenging, frustrating, constructive, demands resolution
Opposition	180 °	☍	Red	Polarizing, at odds, tug of war, push-pull, projection/mirror, needs balance and integration
Quincunx	150 °	⚻	Green	Strained, awkward, uncomfortable, compulsion, mission/problem to solve

If your natal Jupiter is **conjunct** another planet in your chart (or point, ie. Ascendant, Midheaven, Nodes, Chiron and other asteroids if you work with them), what that planet or point represents will feel VERY BIG to you. That energy will be profoundly intertwined with your sense of personal growth, soul purpose, ideals and happiness. A conjunction amplifies, and Jupiter itself is about expansion, so you may have a tendency to overdo it or go to excess around that planet's energy.

If your natal Jupiter is **sextile** or **trine** (referred to as the "soft" aspects) to a planet in your chart, you might feel a natural ease, optimism, joy, and good fortune around your use of that planet's energy, or that planet may harmoniously support your growth and pursuit of your purpose.

If Jupiter is in a **square**, **opposition** or **quincunx** (referred to as "hard" aspects) to planets in your chart, you might feel frustrated, challenged or torn between competing energies that feel at odds with your vision, ideals, purpose and success. You might feel unlucky around that energy, or like there is always some obstacle blocking you. I often describe the square to clients as that feeling of having a pebble in your shoe - it's just irritating, uncomfortable and you want to get it out. I often describe an opposition as a tug of war, or a mirror holding up an opposite reflection through which you see and understand yourself. Ultimately, the challenge of hard aspects is to push you to create change, resolution and integration. Hard aspects to Jupiter may be where you have big lessons to learn.

Minor aspects, like the biquintile, semi-sextile and semi-square, have a lesser effect and impact and are beyond the scope of this book, but feel free to choose to include them if you are more advanced.

Reference Table of Aspect Relationships
Between Signs

Sign	Trine	Square	Opposition
Aries	Leo, Sagittarius	Cancer, Capricorn	Libra
Taurus	Virgo, Capricorn	Leo, Aquarius	Scorpio
Gemini	Libra, Aquarius	Virgo, Pisces	Sagittarius
Cancer	Scorpio, Pisces	Aries, Libra	Capricorn
Leo	Aries, Sagittarius	Taurus, Scorpio	Aquarius
Virgo	Taurus, Capricorn	Gemini, Sagittarius	Pisces
Libra	Gemini, Aquarius	Cancer, Capricorn	Aries
Scorpio	Cancer, Pisces	Leo, Aquarius	Taurus
Sagittarius	Aries, Leo	Virgo, Pisces	Gemini
Capricorn	Taurus, Virgo	Aries, Libra	Cancer
Aquarius	Gemini, Libra	Scorpio, Taurus	Leo
Pisces	Cancer, Scorpio	Gemini, Sagittarius	Virgo

Additionally, though not shown in the table above, the sextile signs are 60 degrees and 2 signs apart, and the quincunx signs are 150 degrees and 5 signs apart.

A note about choosing "Orbs" of Influence when considering aspects:

Planets in your chart sometimes relate to each other in the same exact degree. For instance, you may have a conjunction of Jupiter and Mercury in exactly 14 degrees of Aquarius, or your Jupiter at 14 degrees of Aquarius may be in an exact square to your Sun at 14 degrees of Taurus. But even if two planets don't share the same exact degree, they still influence each other in a meaningful way from several degrees apart to either side. This distance of degrees within which planets are still considered to influence each other in a meaningful way is called an "orb."

The "tighter" the orb, the more powerful the effect and impact. When the two planets touch in the exact degree, that is the most powerful aspect. Within 1-3 degrees is very powerful, but with each degree away, the intensity of the connection weakens. Different astrologers use different orbs when interpreting charts. Orbs may range from 1 degree to 10 degrees for natal planet aspects, with the Sun and Moon (the two great luminaries and major archetypal players of who you are) having the biggest range of up to 10 degrees. Orb ranges differ based on the planets involved (inner, outer, or transpersonal), the type of aspect (major or minor) and for transiting planets that are applying (ie. moving closer to and approaching) or separating (ie. moving past and away from) the natal planet in question. Some astrologers allow as much as a 15 degree aspect when considering the slowest-moving transpersonal planets Uranus, Neptune and Pluto. Robert Pelletier's 1974 seminal book *Planets in Aspect: Understanding Your Inner Dynamics* suggests a planet (for our purposes, Jupiter) to be in major aspect to your natal Sun, Moon or Ascendant if it is within an orb of +/- 8 degrees, and to be in major aspect to any other natal planet within an orb of +/- 6 degrees.

If you are a more seasoned astrologer or student of astrology, I invite you to choose the orbs you are comfortable working with. If you are a complete beginner using Astro.com to calculate your chart, just work with the default orbs in their chart calculation tool.

Now that we've gotten the math and geometry talk out of the way, let's put this into actual use by figuring out what planets and points are in relationship to your Jupiter, and most importantly, what you understand that to mean for yourself.

Truth be told, this has been the most challenging and complicated chapter for me to write. As an astrologer and coach, I try my best to help my clients piece together the complex puzzle of their planetary placements in a holistic way that has direct application to their life. Planetary signs (like we addressed in Chapter 3) and planetary houses (like we addressed in Chapter 4) are more straightforward and easier to make sense of for a beginner than planetary aspects -- like the difference between doing a 100-piece puzzle and a 1000 piece puzzle.

In this chapter, I have attempted to simplify this very complex and dynamic topic into accessible and practical terms that you can use to understand your Jupiterian nature. But I have also been careful not to over-simplify or dumb-down the nature of aspects by blatantly characterizing some aspects as "good" and "positive" and others as "bad" or "negative." Some astrologers and horoscope apps do this, relating to all trines as easy and all squares and oppositions as bad news. As an astrologer and coach, I don't find absolutism to be true or particularly helpful when you are seeking growth and transformation.

I have come to a deep and humble appreciation that there are potential positives and negatives, benefits and challenges, conscious and shadow expressions of any placement or aspect. So much depends on the client's perspective, awareness, mindset, and beliefs about their inner and outer experience. Any challenge can be a source of new learning, resilience, pride, skillfulness, and accomplishment. Any easy thing in our life can be taken for granted, under-utilized, or keep you stuck in old familiar patterns that don't support your growth.

So instead of giving you a set prescription, I offer you a range of some possible interpretations of how Jupiter in aspect to planets in your birth chart may inform how you understand your higher purpose, ideals, growth, and abundance. These interpretations may resonate for you as they are framed, or in the opposite, absence, or negation of that experience, or somewhere along a spectrum. **As always, I encourage you to trust yourself and your inner guidance.**

Step-by-step suggestions for how to use the Jupiter Aspect worksheets:

1. Identify all Jupiter aspects in your natal chart from the My Natal Jupiter Worksheet in Chapter 2 and record them in the My Jupiter Aspects Worksheet on the next page, for easy access.

2. Use the worksheets that follow in this chapter for those planets or points that your Jupiter is connected to by aspect. Ignore and skip the worksheets for planets that are not in aspect with your Jupiter.

3. In each worksheet that applies to your natal chart, read through the possible ways a connection between Jupiter and that planet may present. You might choose to put an asterisk, checkmark or highlight the expressions that resonate with you as recognizable patterns in your life. You might make notes about your experience next to the statements.

4. If the opposite or negation of one of those expressions is what resonates with you, you might cross out words and change the language (ie. from "does" to "does not", "optimistic" to "pessimistic", "lucky/abundant" to "unlucky/scarce").

5. If a statement feels true for only some moments or experiences of your life, or has changed over time, you might want to make notes about that.

6. You might consider the specific aspect (conjunct, sextile, trine, square, opposition, quincunx) and observe the

ways in which this type of relationship has felt easy or hard, or helped or hindered you in different ways and at different times in your life.

7. You might reflect on the signs and houses Jupiter and the aspected planet are in, to add additional insight about how that energy is working for you. Look back to Chapters 3 and 4 to help you reflect on the meanings of the signs and houses.

8. Finally, I invite you to apply your new insights to reflect on how you might consciously apply and leverage this Jupiter/planet relationship as you move forward towards your dreams, purpose, and goals.

My Jupiter Natal Aspects Worksheets

My natal Jupiter

Degree/Sign _________________ House _________________

is connected to these planets/points by aspect

Planet/ Point	Degree/Sign	Aspect
_____________	_____________	_____________
_____________	_____________	_____________
_____________	_____________	_____________
_____________	_____________	_____________
_____________	_____________	_____________
_____________	_____________	_____________
_____________	_____________	_____________

My Jupiter - Sun Aspect Worksheet

♃ Jupiter   sign ________ degrees ________   house ________

☉ Sun   sign ________ degrees ________   house ________

Jupiter-Sun aspect ________________________

The Sun -- who I am, my core sense of self, identity, outer expression, creativity, vitality, ego, will, where/how I shine, my self-expression, what energizes me

Jupiter - Sun connections may present like:

- I have boundless enthusiasm and faith in myself, my self-expression, and my creative abilities
- I know myself to be a happy, self-confident, optimistic and inspired person
- I strongly identify with my ideals and higher spiritual purpose
- I have an inflated sense of self/ego and to need be seen as the center of attention
- I am energized by growth, learning, exploration, adventure
- I feel blessed, prosperous, and have faith that I can get what I want in life
- I feel unlucky, pessimistic, or like life is thwarting my success
- I struggle with knowing my vision and purpose, or lack faith or vision
- I am frustrated or blocked around my self-expression and creativity
- I lack self-confidence or don't feel able to outwardly shine or express myself
- I grow and expand my self-confidence through overcoming difficult challenges

Reflections on how I have experienced my Jupiter-Sun aspect:

Any other reflections, specific to the nature of the aspect, signs and houses?

How might I consciously apply and leverage my Jupiter/ Sun potential as I move forward towards my dreams, purpose and goals?

My Jupiter - Moon Aspect Worksheet

♃ Jupiter   sign________   degrees ________   house ________

☽ Moon   sign________   degrees________   house ________

Jupiter-Moon aspect ______________________________

The Moon -- how I feel, my emotions, my innermost needs, my emotional responses, what I need to feel safe and protected, my connection to home, family, parents, and myself as a parent

<u>Jupiter -- Moon connections may present like:</u>

- I feel very protective, generous and nurturing towards my family and loved ones
- My default emotional response is enthusiastic, faithful, positive and optimistic
- I have a big need to feel connected to a higher spiritual/ soul purpose
- I am very emotionally sensitive, intuitive and/or empathic
- I have a big need for travel, adventure, higher learning and/or wisdom-seeking
- I can be overly reactive or struggle to manage my emotions
- My inner needs, self-care and self-love feel really important
- I feel pessimistic or unlucky about having my needs met
- I resist growth and learning that challenges me to move out of my comfort zone
- My relationship with my mother, or being a mother/parent, is a big theme in my life
- My sense of responsibility to home and family are in congruence with or in conflict with my hopes and dreams

Reflections on how I have experienced my Jupiter-Moon aspect:

Any other reflections, specific to the nature of the aspect, signs and houses?

How might I consciously apply and leverage my Jupiter/ Moon potential as I move forward towards my dreams, purpose and goals?

My Jupiter - Ascendant Aspect Worksheet

♃ Jupiter   sign _________   degrees ________   house_________

AC Ascendant sign_________   degrees_________   house _________

Jupiter-Ascendant aspect _______________________

Ascendant -- my outer personality, the role I play, how other people see me, the image I project, my physical appearance, my individual approach to life and lifestyle

<u>Jupiter -- Ascendant connections may present like:</u>
- I have a BIG personality and larger than life presence
- I have a faithful, optimistic, happy-go-lucky personality and approach to life
- Travel, adventure, growth and truth-seeking are central to how I live my life
- I identify with the role of spiritual guide, motivator, influencer, guru or philosopher
- Others view me as an inspiring and positive influence and/or person of high ethical and moral beliefs
- I struggle to find alignment between the roles others expect me to play and my own sense of soul purpose and vision
- The way I live my life feels at odds or in conflict with what brings me a sense of joy, possibility and optimism
- I have an inflated ego and am overly absorbed with myself, my appearance, or the impression others have of me
- I may be pompous and overly moralistic about my ideas and truths
- My physical body may be large

Reflections on how I have experienced my Jupiter-Ascendant aspect:

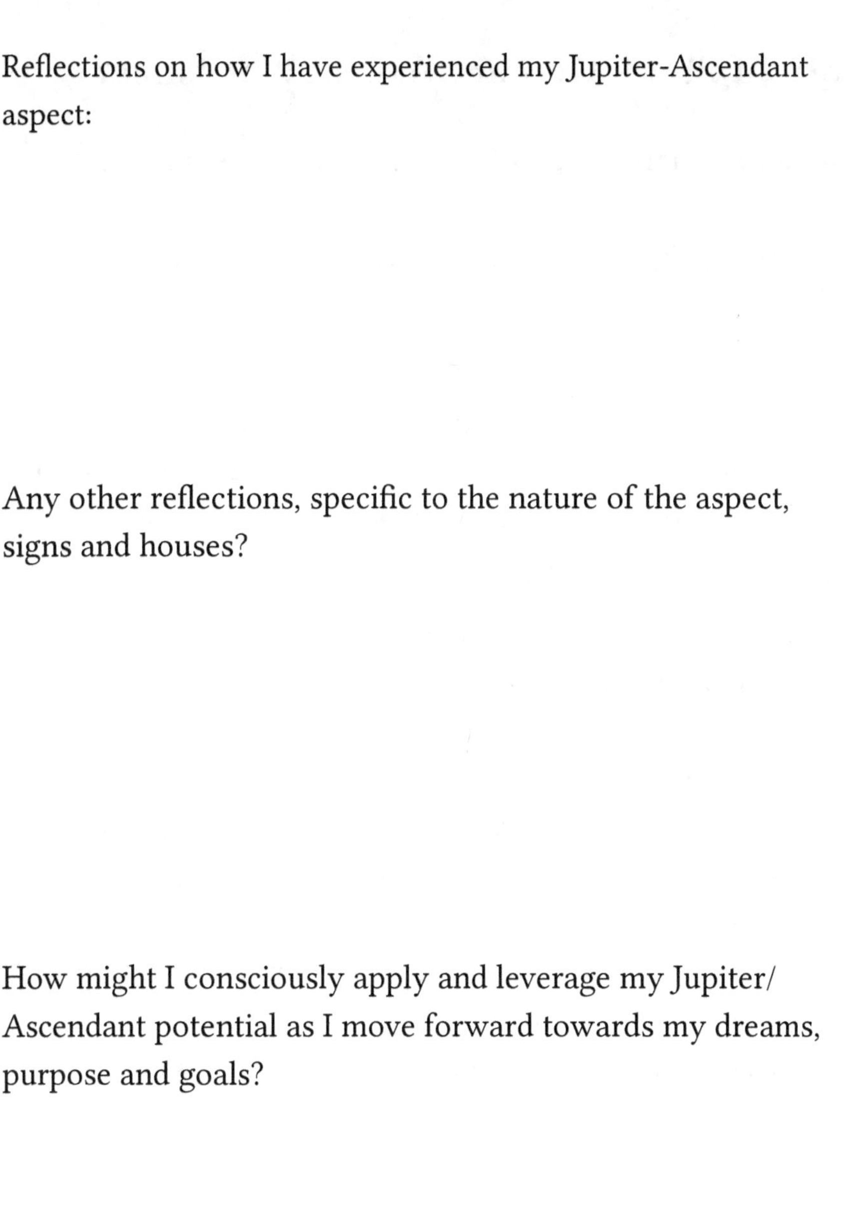

Any other reflections, specific to the nature of the aspect, signs and houses?

How might I consciously apply and leverage my Jupiter/ Ascendant potential as I move forward towards my dreams, purpose and goals?

My Jupiter - Mercury Aspect Worksheet

♃ Jupiter   sign________ degrees_________   house _________

♀ Mercury sign________   degrees_________   house_________

Jupiter-Mercury aspect _______________________

Mercury -- how I think, learn, communicate, how my mind and intellect work, what I am curious about, my physical agility and movement, my nervous system, adaptability, versatility

<u>Jupiter -- Mercury connections may present like:</u>
- I have a very big mental and intellectual capacity for learning, thinking and communicating
- I feel happy, purposeful and expansive about learning, taking in new information, growing in knowledge, and teaching
- My mind is overactive, easily distracted and/or prone to excessive thinking, ruminating and fluctuating between ideas
- I may be excessively talkative or seek constant social stimulation and conversation
- I have an insatiable curiosity and seek to understand a wide expanse of things
- I have an overactive or highly sensitive nervous system and need constant movement
- I feel inspired and lucky in my physical body's agility and capacity for movement and athletics
- I am naturally adept with language and musical pursuits
- I feel challenged around learning, speaking, reading or writing

Reflections on how I have experienced my Jupiter-Mercury aspect:

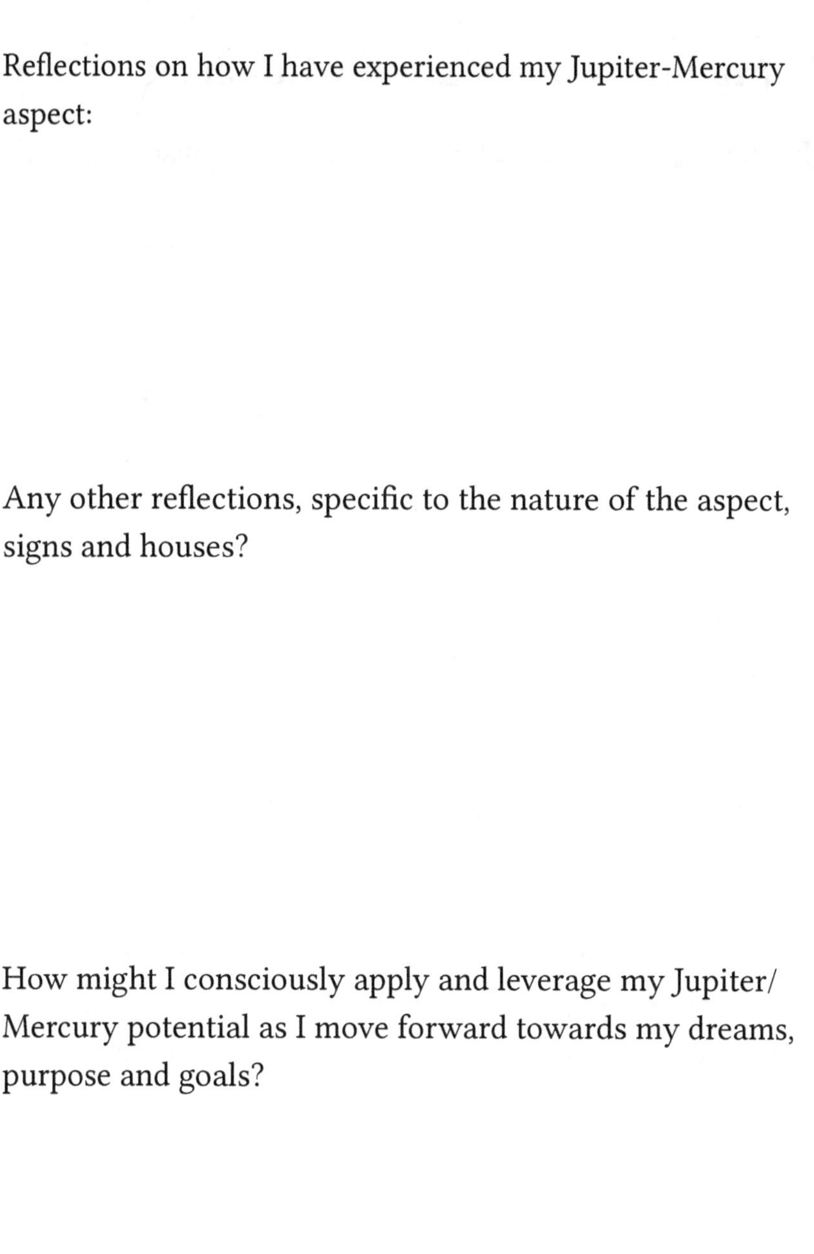

Any other reflections, specific to the nature of the aspect, signs and houses?

How might I consciously apply and leverage my Jupiter/ Mercury potential as I move forward towards my dreams, purpose and goals?

My Jupiter - Venus Aspect Worksheet

♃ Jupiter   sign________   degrees________   house ________

♀ Venus   sign ________   degrees ________   house ________

Jupiter-Venus aspect ____________________________

Venus -- what I find beautiful and value, my love language, how I give/receive affection and pleasure, what/who I am attracted to, money, possessions, resources, skills, food, Nature

<u>Jupiter -- Venus connections may present like:</u>

- Beauty, harmony, and physical pleasure are hugely important values for me on a soul level
- I give love in an expansive, open, faithful, and abundant way
- I feel challenged or unlucky in love and relationships
- I feel fortunate to have an abundance of intimate connections with friends, sisters and/or lovers
- I value and invest in my personal growth, spirituality and wisdom-seeking
- I love adventure and new experiences, especially involving art, beauty, and travel
- My vision and ideals may be at odds with or create strain in my relationships with people and/or money
- I may be over-indulgent and prone to excess around material comforts, food, money, sensual pleasure
- I may feel especially blessed or thwarted around financial abundance and security

Reflections on how I have experienced my Jupiter-Venus aspect:

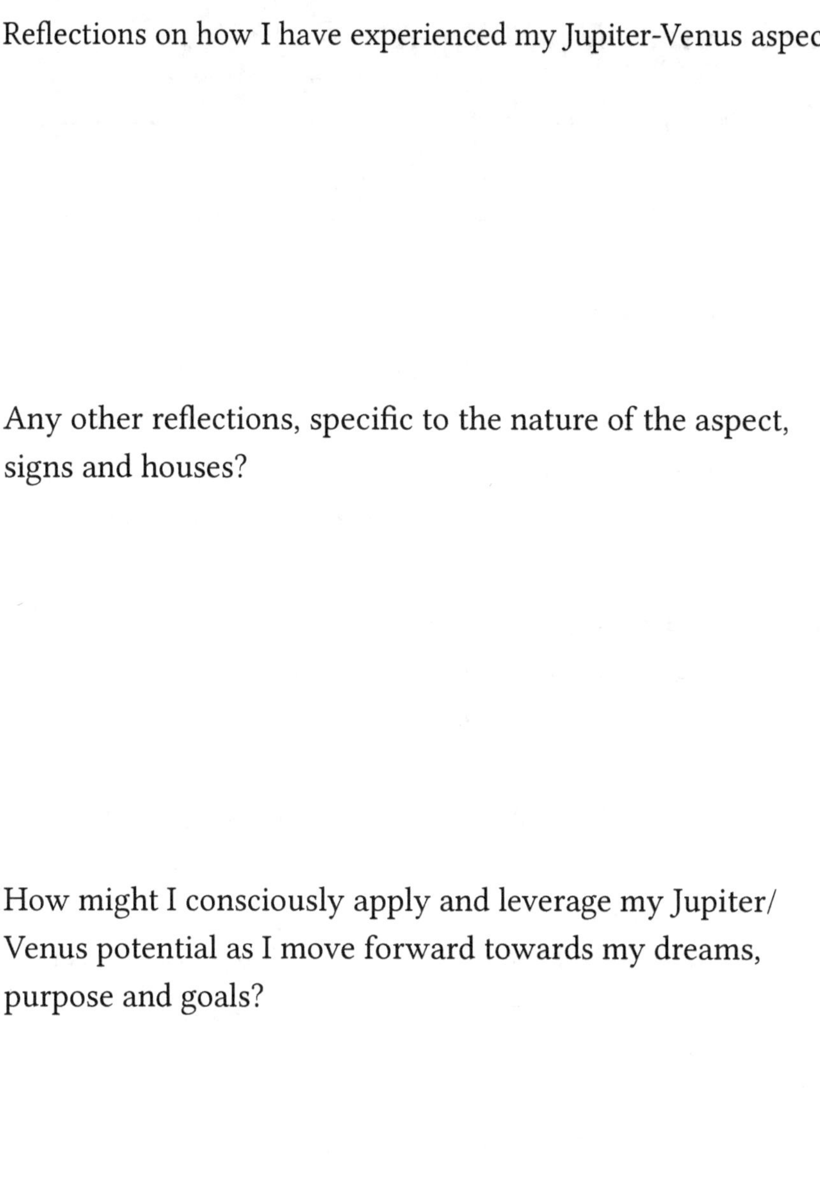

Any other reflections, specific to the nature of the aspect, signs and houses?

How might I consciously apply and leverage my Jupiter/ Venus potential as I move forward towards my dreams, purpose and goals?

My Jupiter - Mars Aspect Worksheet

♃ Jupiter   sign________ degrees________   house ________

♂ Mars   sign________ degrees________   house ________

Jupiter-Mars aspect ________________________

Mars -- what I desire and passionate about, my physical vitality, my sexual drive, where I am competitive, goal-oriented, what I am willing to fight for, courage, boldness, assertiveness, aggression, anger, impulsivity, risk-taking, violence

Jupiter -- Mars connections may present like:

- I have big dreams and ambitions I want to achieve
- I have a strong desire for self-improvement, personal growth and accomplishment
- I have abundant energy and drive to be in active pursuit of my ideals
- I have strong, bold, masculine, warrior energy
- I feel impatient, volatile or easily triggered to anger or violence
- I am prone to excessive impulsivity, risk-taking and adventure-seeking
- I act with boldness, confidence, and directness
- I feel blocked or don't have the energy or confidence to pursue what makes me happy or feels meaningful on a soul level
- I can be overly competitive or aggressive when I don't win or when my ideals or visions are challenged
- I am strongly sexual or may struggle with sex, sexuality, or sexual desire/urges
- I feel blessed in my athletic and physical ability

Reflections on how I have experienced my Jupiter-Mars aspect:

Any other reflections, specific to the nature of the aspect, signs and houses?

How might I consciously apply and leverage my Jupiter/ Mars potential as I move forward towards my dreams, purpose and goals?

My Jupiter - Saturn Aspect Worksheet

♃ Jupiter sign_________ degrees_________ house _________

♄ Saturn sign _________ degrees_________ house _________

Jupiter-Saturn aspect _______________________

Saturn -- what I work hard at, take seriously and commit to, where I apply self-discipline, boundaries, and rules, maturity and adulthood, what I seek to manifest/accomplish, legacy, fear of failure, mastery, authority, patience, responsibility, tradition

<u>Jupiter -- Saturn connections may present like:</u>

- I have an abundance of discipline to work hard and persevere to accomplish my dreams and vision
- I take myself, my success, authority and status very seriously
- I have a big fear of failure and resist putting effort into what I don't think I will succeed at
- I have boundless patience to work steadily towards long-range goals and mastery
- I seek to grow and improve myself (and my body) through slow, methodical, strategic, long-term effort
- My need to expand and grow is often limited by my need for stability and structure
- My fear, negativity, or sense of responsibility interferes with my spontaneous joy, adventure or optimism
- I have faith that my hard work will merit reward and prosperity
- My caution is in conflict with my imagination
- Being a responsible adult or in a position of authority is a big part of my purpose

Reflections on how I have experienced my Jupiter-Saturn aspect:

Any other reflections, specific to the nature of the aspect, signs and houses?

How might I consciously apply and leverage my Jupiter/ Saturn potential as I move forward towards my dreams, purpose and goals?

My Jupiter - Uranus Aspect Worksheet

♃ Jupiter sign________ degrees________ house ________

♅ Uranus sign________ degrees________ house________

Jupiter-Uranus aspect _______________________

Uranus -- my uniqueness, how/where I seek freedom and authenticity, non-conformity, unexpected changes, flashes of insight, rebellion, eccentricity, futuristic-minded, humanitarianism, progress, innovation

<u>Jupiter -- Uranus connections may present like:</u>

- I have a big need for freedom, individuality, and uniqueness
- I have sudden flashes of vision/inspiration/insight/wisdom
- I have many non-conforming, unconventional beliefs
- I proudly identify as LGBTQ+
- I grow and learn through sudden, unexpected changes of good or bad fortune in my life
- I am idealistic and optimistic for the future of humanity, innovation and social advances, or I struggle with pessimism about humanity and the future
- I aspire to travel and experience new places, cultures, and people
- I struggle with faith that change will be positive or lead to my success and happiness
- My rebelliousness or refusal to submit to conventional rules creates an obstacle to my abundance and growth
- I feel unlucky, pessimistic or victimized by sudden unexpected disruptions and upheavals in my life

Reflections on how I have experienced my Jupiter-Uranus aspect:

Any other reflections, specific to the nature of the aspect, signs and houses?

How might I consciously apply and leverage my Jupiter/ Uranus potential as I move forward towards my dreams, purpose and goals?

My Jupiter - Neptune Aspect Worksheet

♃ Jupiter   sign________ degrees________   house ________

♆ Neptune sign________ degrees ________   house________

Jupiter-Neptune aspect ________________________

Neptune -- my faith, spirituality and connection to Soul, my intuition and empathy, creativity and imagination, transcendence and union with a higher power, fantasy, dreams, surrender, merging/co-dependence, illusion/disillusionment, addictions, meditation/mysticism, yoga

Jupiter -- Neptune connections may present like:

- I have big aspirations around connecting and merging with Oneness, transcendence, and higher consciousness
- I get lost in my imagination and fantasies
- I have a big need to escape reality
- I can overly idealize/romanticize people or experiences, and can be gullible, easily deceived or disillusioned
- I feel faithful and trusting in Life and a higher purpose
- I am extremely empathic, intuitive, psychic, or emotionally sensitive
- I feel blessed and lucky around my innate talent for music, art, or imagination
- I seek wisdom and higher spiritual truths beyond "ordinary" reality
- I live with my head in the clouds, procrastinate and struggle with day-to-day responsibilities
- My addictions or compulsive escapist behaviors are at odds with my success and living into my soul purpose

Reflections on how I have experienced my Jupiter-Neptune aspect:

Any other reflections, specific to the nature of the aspect, signs and houses?

How might I consciously apply and leverage my Jupiter/ Neptune potential as I move forward towards my dreams, purpose and goals?

My Jupiter - Pluto Aspect Worksheet

♃ Jupiter   sign _________ degrees_________   house _________

♀ Pluto   sign _________ degrees _________   house _________

Jupiter-Pluto aspect _______________________

Pluto -- how I transform/evolve through crisis/loss/death, power/disempowerment, resilience, resurrection, "dark night of the soul" experiences, rebirth, secrecy, control, shadow/ depth psychology, mental health struggles/depression, wealth and power

Jupiter -- Pluto connections may present like:

- I have faith and optimism around transformational processes
- I have ideals and aspirations around my own power, evolution, and resilience
- Death, loss, power/control, sex, and/or abuse are big important themes in my life
- I feel unlucky or pessimistic about the painful, dark shadow aspects of myself, others and my experience of the world
- My biggest growth and learning comes from overcoming challenging losses, death, abuse or mental health struggles
- I have ideals around transformational psychology
- I feel suspicious, secretive, or untrusting of other people's agendas in joint ventures and relationships
- I am blessed with abundant wealth and prosperity through my inheritance or the power I have wielded
- I learn and grow through relationships characterized by power struggle

Reflections on how I have experienced my Jupiter-Pluto aspect:

Any other reflections, specific to the nature of the aspect, signs and houses?

How might I consciously apply and leverage my Jupiter/ Pluto potential as I move forward towards my dreams, purpose and goals?

My Jupiter - Midheaven Aspect Worksheet

♃ Jupiter   sign_________   degrees_________   house_________

MC Midheaven sign_________   degrees_________   house_________

Jupiter-Midheaven aspect ______________________

Midheaven -- what I am being guided to accomplish at my highest potential, how I actualize my skills and talents through my profession, my public reputation and status, how I can best contribute to society and the world

<u>Jupiter -- Midheaven connections may present like:</u>

- I have aspirations, a calling and a sense of purpose around doing something great out in the world through my professional vocation
- I feel successful, prosperous, and blessed in my ability to live into my highest potential through my chosen work in the world
- I have big goals to achieve recognition, fame, acclaim or status in a public way
- My spiritual ideals and truths are in conflict with my professional goals
- I feel unlucky or thwarted around career success, or lack faith that I will gain due recognition for my accomplishments
- Higher law, justice, philosophy, spirituality, academia, teaching or ethics are integral to my chosen career path
- My spiritual beliefs and ethics do not find meaningful expression in my professional path
- I am happiest and most optimistic when I am contributing my wisdom for the greater good

Reflections on how I have experienced my
Jupiter-Midheaven aspect:

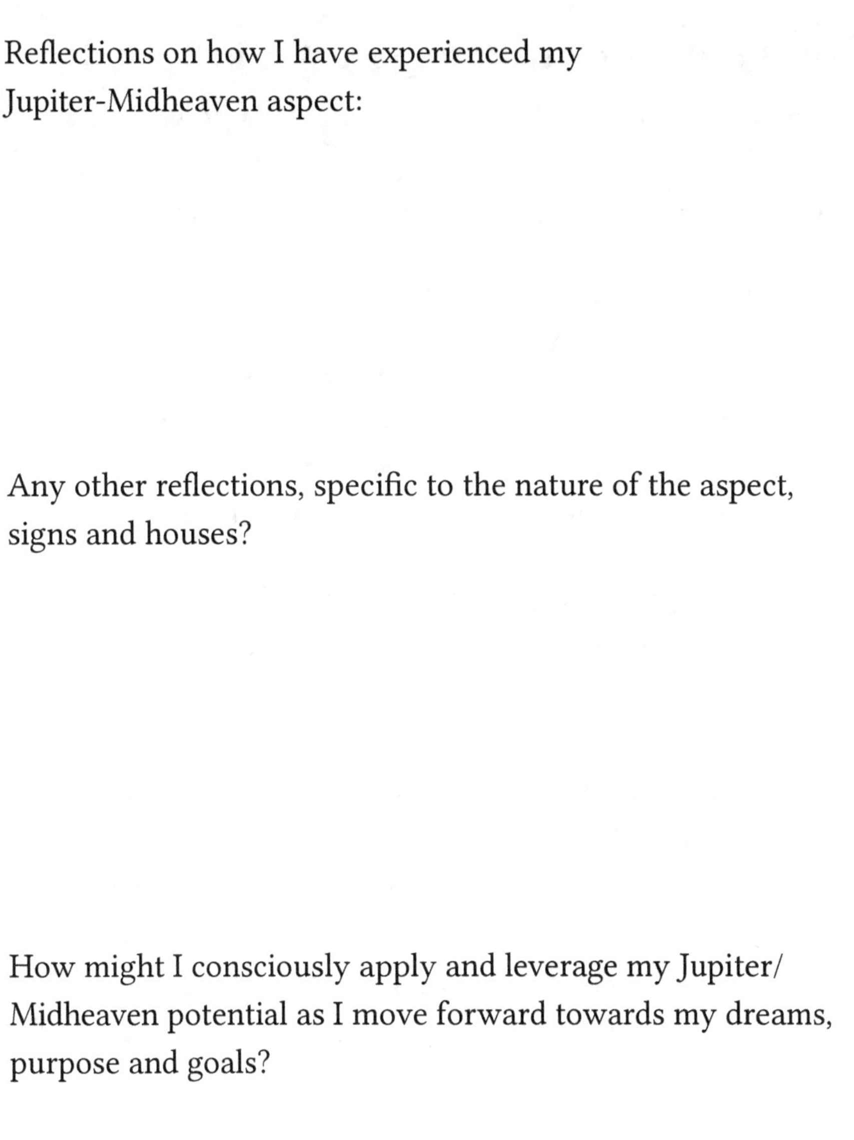

Any other reflections, specific to the nature of the aspect,
signs and houses?

How might I consciously apply and leverage my Jupiter/
Midheaven potential as I move forward towards my dreams,
purpose and goals?

My Jupiter - Chiron Aspect Worksheet

♃ Jupiter   sign________   degrees________   house ________

⚷ Chiron   sign________   degrees________   house ________

Jupiter-Chiron aspect _____________________

Chiron - the "wounded healer," where I have a wound/feel inadequate/insecure/not enough, physical and emotional health issues, where I heal to love and accept myself as an integrated whole, where I am a healer/mentor/guide to others

<u>Jupiter -- Chiron connections may present like:</u>

- I have a strong sense of soul calling and purpose around being a teacher, healer or mentor
- I am faithful, trusting and optimistic about the potential to heal wounds and attain wholeness and integration
- I feel lucky and blessed around my health
- I feel a sense of inadequacy, insecurity, or not being good enough
- I feel challenged or unlucky about my health, or victimized by chronic or serious bouts of illness
- I have limiting beliefs about my worth or ability to receive abundance and prosperity
- I seek spiritual meaning and adopt an expansive growth-mindset to heal myself and contribute to others' healing
- I have aspirations around travel, experiencing new places and cultures, as a way to heal my connection to my own soul, to others, and to my higher purpose
- I grow and expand myself through seeking mentorship or becoming a mentor

Reflections on how I have experienced my Jupiter-Chiron aspect:

Any other reflections, specific to the nature of the aspect, signs and houses?

How might I consciously apply and leverage my Jupiter/ Chiron potential as I move forward towards my dreams, purpose and goals?

My Jupiter - Nodal Aspect Worksheet

♃ Jupiter   sign________   degrees__________   house ________

☋ South Node sign________   degrees________   house ________

☊ North Node sign________   degrees_______   house________

Jupiter-South Node aspect ____________________________

Jupiter-North Node aspect ____________________________

(Note: The Nodes are not physical objects in space, but astronomical points calculated based on the intersection of the Moon's orbit around Earth with the Earth's orbit around the Sun.)

South Node -- what my soul came into this life already knowing, past life's experience, karma, what feels familiar and comfortable to me, innate talents and skills, patterns I repeat over and over, habits I need to break or grow beyond in this lifetime

North Node - what my soul came into this life to learn and grow around, this life's lessons, dharma, what feels unfamiliar and out of my comfort zone, what challenges me, what I am growing into, what I feel "destined" to learn and accomplish on a soul level

Jupiter -- Nodal connections may present like:

- I feel faithful and idealist about personal growth, soul purpose, and spirituality
- I feel optimistic, blessed and prosperous around my ability to apply my innate gifts and talents in a way that grows me into new and challenging experiences
- I feel challenged by or continually repeat unconscious or subconscious patterns and habits that interfere with my growth
- Facing what is hard or uncomfortable feels very purposeful and is deeply connected to my sense of soul growth and truth
- My ideals and visions feel aligned with or out of sync with my natural talents or the life lessons I am feeling pushed to learn

Reflections on how I have experienced my Jupiter-South Node aspect:

Any other reflections, specific to the nature of the aspect, signs and houses?

How might I consciously apply and leverage my Jupiter/South Node potential as I move forward towards my dreams, purpose and goals?

Reflections on how I have experienced my Jupiter-North
Node aspect:

Any other reflections, specific to the nature of the aspect,
signs and houses?

How might I consciously apply and leverage my Jupiter/
North Node potential as I move forward towards my dreams,
purpose and goals?

Chapter 6: My Jupiter Cycles

Jupiter's movement through the entire zodiac takes approx-imately twelve years -- (11 years 10-½ months to be more accurate). Since there are twelve signs and twelve houses of the zodiac, this means that Jupiter spends approximately one full year in a given sign. It also means that Jupiter, in that given sign, spends approximately one full year impacting and growing you in the area of one to two houses in your chart where you have that sign.

According to Steven Arroyo, "You could throw out all the rest of astrology and, just by using Jupiter and Saturn passing through or "transiting" your natal houses, you would have such a practical tool that it would be better than any other method I know for understanding the cyclic and regular nature of important developments, changes, and growth periods in your life." *Relationships and Life Cycles*, p. 186

This chapter will give you the practical tools and resources to work with understanding the cycles of Jupiter transits in your life. I am writing a book on Saturn next, to help you explore important Saturn archetypes and cycles of coming into responsibility, accomplishment, and maturity, so stay tuned for that.

Transits and Free Will

Wherever Jupiter is moving through your chart, there is an impulse and urge to grow and improve yourself, expand wisdom, have new experiences, envision what is possible, create meaning, and connect with spiritual purpose and values. Jupiter transits expand your optimism, hope, and faith about new opportunities presented in that area of your life. Depending on what other planets Jupiter is in aspect with during a given transit, you may experience more positive or challenging expressions of those energies. A Jupiter transit may bring abundance, prosperity, generosity, and joy, or it may feel like you are challenged around these gifts, or over-indulging in the area of your life being impacted by the transit.

According to astrologer Robert Hand, "Transits indicate times that are appropriate for certain kinds of actions and inappropriate for others, and certain kinds of events often do occur with particular transits. But transits should never be viewed as signifying events that will inevitably come to pass, with you as a helpless observer." *Planets in Transit*, p. 3

As a humanistic and evolutionary astrologer and a transformational life coach, I believe humans have free will. Astrological transits do not fatalistically predetermine the events and outcomes of your life. How you choose to work with planetary transits is largely up to you. Understanding your personal astrology is like having a cosmic GPS that helps you see where you are on your life path, what's on the road, what alternate routes you might choose, and how you might best navigate to where you want to be heading. Astrology is the guidance system, but you are in the driver's seat of your life.

Astrology helps us reclaim our free will. Instead of feeling like a lucky or unlucky pawn in life's game, or a victim of other people or of our circumstances, astrology provides context and perspective that helps us choose how we relate to our experience, and what we make it mean. Jupiter transit cycles are not "acting on us" as much as they are an invitation to bring awareness to how and where we have ideals, aspire to connect to meaning and personal purpose, and seek to acquire new wisdom. Jupiterian cycles present us with opportunities to grow, evolve, and become more aligned with our higher purpose and fulfillment.

My Jupiter Returns

Your "Jupiter return" occurs approximately every twelve years when Jupiter comes back to the same position, by sign and degree, as your natal Jupiter. Whatever sign Jupiter was in when you were born, it will return to that sign again when you are around age 12, 24, 36, 48, 60, 72, 84, and onward. Are some key life experiences from those years already jumping out at you? Great! That's what you will be exploring in this section with the My Jupiter Return(s) Worksheet.

According to astrologer Alexander Ruperti, "The rhythm of Jupiter return cycles will describe, in a potentially ascending spiral, an individual's attempt to grow toward being "more than an individual." They express the urge to expand not merely outward but upward as well. Each new

Jupiter cycle is potentially more than a simple repetition of the last... Each of these seven cycles, having its own significant meaning and purpose, will be an important turning point in the life of an individual....What becomes possible at these times is the use of the Jupiter energy in a new and different way that will affect one's relationship to society and one's participation in it." -- *Cycles of Becoming*, p.117-118

****

What purpose is my soul aiming at and growing toward?

****

The My Jupiter Return(s) Worksheet will prompt you to remember and reflect on what your soul was aiming at and growing toward at each Jupiter return, when you were 12, 24, and so on. The intention of these reflections is to help you arrive at new clarity and insight about your personal growth and purpose, in an ascending spiral through your life.

In the interest of space, I am only providing one template of the worksheet in this physical book. You might choose to reflect on all ages simultaneously on the single worksheet provided in the book but will likely need additional space. Appendix E offers blank extra journal pages for you to use as overflow reflection space. Alternatively, I suggest you use a separate worksheet for each Jupiter return (ie. one for age 12, one for age 24, and so on) in which case you will need to make copies or download the .pdf file of the worksheet to print or work with on your computer. Find the process that works best for you.

To assist you in easily locating the years Jupiter was traveling through your natal sign, I have provided a full reference in Appendix C to the date ranges when Jupiter was in each zodiac sign. If you are a complete beginner, you can just work with the whole year of Jupiter returning to your sign. Actually, the worksheets guide everyone to do that anyway, since memories you have are likely to be over the broader time frame of that year anyway.

But as we discussed in Chapter 5 about aspects and orbs, transiting Jupiter isn't creating a powerful conjunction to your natal Jupiter for the entire year it is moving through that sign. It is at its most potent influence when it is within 0-3 degrees of your natal Jupiter (or up to 6 or 10 degrees, depending on the orb you are comfortable working with). For instance, if your natal Jupiter is in 8 degrees of Cancer, you might consider your Jupiter return timing to be when Jupiter was moving through 5 to 11 degrees of Cancer. The added benefit of identifying a tighter date range for your Jupiter return is that sometimes big impactful events and growth experiences will have occurred right in the time window of the close conjunction. These key times may feel like "turning points" as Ruperti expressed. Knowing this can be very validating, affirming, and add another layer of understanding about how Jupiter is operating in your life. It can also help you plan and create intentional awareness during the timing of your next Jupiter return.

If you would like to identify the more exact and potent time frame of your Jupiter returns, you will need to use an ephemeris book, a free online ephemeris, astrology software, or consult a professional astrologer. In Appendix B, I provide easy step-by-step instructions on how to use a free online ephemeris.

Remember that your natal Jupiter is connected to, influenced by, and influences other planets in your birth chart that it has an aspect relationship with. In Chapter 5, you identified those connections and reflected on how you have experienced them. Every twelve years, during your Jupiter return, those other planets are also being called into action by transiting Jupiter's connection with them. So, while the conjunction to your natal Jupiter is the main character of your Jupiter return show, the worksheet will prompt you to integrate an awareness of the effect of transiting Jupiter forming trines, squares, and/or oppositions to other planets in your chart as it passes over your natal Jupiter, since they are other characters intertwined with your soul's story.

<u>Here are some suggestions that may help your process</u>:
- talk with family or friends who knew you at each return age and can help you remember events and stories
- look through old photos and mementos from that age and year
- meditate, pray, dream or create ritual to evoke revelation and insight about how you were growing and becoming at that age
- create art or doodle images related to memories and themes that show up
- listen to music from that year and age and pay attention to feelings and memories that are stirred up
- work at your own pace

- trust and be compassionate with yourself

An important caution about working with memories: If you have survived serious traumatic past events, please be responsible about deciding whether or not to revisit that trauma in these exercises, and how to engage with memory in a safe way that does not cause you harm. This book is not offering therapy or professional mental health guidance. Please seek out a licensed therapist or other medical professional to support your well-being, as needed.

As you connect with your memories, the worksheets invite you to stay in the present moment with whatever you are noticing now. This is absolutely key to unlocking new perspectives and reframing old stories into inspiring and healing narratives that support you now. You are re-visiting the past, in this present moment, with the aim of becoming a wiser, happier, more powerful version of yourself as you move into the future.

It is my hope and belief that going through this self-reflective process you will arrive at a deeper understanding and appreciation of your life's growth trajectory up to this point. This new awareness can be applied to your upcoming future Jupiter returns, so you can align with and maximize your potential for satisfaction, meaning and joy.

My Jupiter Return(s) Worksheet

My Natal Jupiter Sign and Degrees_______________________

Using Appendix C, record below the year(s) that Jupiter returned to your natal Jupiter sign, and your age at that return

(year in sign - year of my birth = age at return)

Year/Date range Jupiter returned to my natal sign:

My Age:

More precise date range of Jupiter return

____

(optional, referencing an ephemeris and +/-____°orb, see Appendix B)

Important memories of myself, people, and events in my life at that time:

What interests was I enthusiastically pursuing, learning, and growing around?

What brought me the greatest joy? What did I feel optimistic, hopeful, and full of possibility about?

What were my dreams and ideals at that time? Did I have a vision or aim for my future? What was it?

Is there something I felt lucky or abundant about?

Was I going to excess or extremes around anything
at that age?

What were my core beliefs, philosophies, or spiritual
pursuits at that age?

Looking at my Jupiter house placement and the work I did
in Chapter 4, how was I growing around that house's themes
during my Jupiter return? What aspirations, growth, faith,
or abundance did I experience in that area of my life?

Looking at my Jupiter aspects and the work I did in Chapter 5, how was Jupiter amplifying, supporting or challenging other planetary energies during my Jupiter return? In what ways were these other planetary energies helping or hindering me in my growth, vision, faith or abundance at that time?

What new awareness have I arrived at through this reflection exercise? What are my takeaways about my Jupiter return?

How do I want to apply this new learning as I move forward into who I am becoming and what I intend to accomplish next?

My Jupiter Sign and House Cycles_

Just as Jupiter returns to a conjunction with your natal Jupiter in its sign and house approximately every twelve years, it will also return to each of the other eleven signs and houses in your chart on a twelve-year cycle. Each year of your life, Jupiter's energy is influencing you in a unique and individual way, with the aim of expanding you through growth lessons in a given area of your life. The My Jupiter Sign and House Cycles Worksheet is designed to help you explore how Jupiter has grown and expanded you, in a cyclical way, each time it was in each zodiac sign and location in your chart.

For instance, Jupiter in Pisces in the universe will have a specific energy of expanding Piscean themes for everyone in a more global way. But in your own life, Jupiter in Pisces might be moving through your 6th and 7th houses, and aspecting your Moon and Mars. The dynamic changes and experiences this energy creates for you, and how you interact with and learn from it, is very specific and individual to you.

I frequently walk clients through Jupiter return cycle exercises. I can't emphasize enough how valuable it is to look back 12, 24, 36 years ago from the moment you (and Jupiter) are situated in, to glean insight into your evolution and possibility. I am confident you will have lots of "a-ha!" revelations when you do this exercise.

Looking back at the Reference Table of Aspect Relationships Between Signs in Chapter 5 (pg. 89) can help you identify what other planets any given Jupiter transit is awakening. For instance, every twelve years when Jupiter makes a trip through Pisces, it will at some point during that year:

- form a conjunction with any planets or points you have in Pisces
- form a trine with planets or points you have in Cancer or Scorpio
- form as square with planets or points you have in Gemini or Sagittarius
- form an opposition with planet or points you have in Virgo

Also take a look at the sign your natal Jupiter is in, and what signs are trine, square or opposing that sign. Whenever Jupiter in the universe is moving through one of those signs, it will connect back to your natal Jupiter in an important way that you can also bring awareness to.

For instance, as I write this book, Jupiter is in Aries in the universe. I can look to previous Jupiter in Aries cycles in my life 12, 24 and 36 years ago, and so on. Jupiter's transit through Aries happens for me in my first house where I also have my North Node, Chiron, Venus and Saturn, all in Aries. Transiting Jupiter in Aries opposes my natal Jupiter (aka, a Jupiter opposition), Uranus and South Node in Libra in my 7th house. I want to understand what all of that might mean for me! So I worked through the My Jupiter Sign and House Cycles Worksheet and got so much valuable insight and perspective. I made brand new connections that led me to consciously lean into prioritizing my own independence, goals, and relationship with myself this year – like spending more time on my own, doing the things I want to do, and writing a book!

<u>Here are some suggestions on how you might use the Jupiter Sign and House Cycles Worksheet</u>:

1. Explore your cycles around the sign where Jupiter is currently in the universe. This will help you look back at your life story and past patterns around Jupiter in this sign and house so you can apply the insights you glean to the present.

2. Explore your cycles around the sign where Jupiter was last year. That will help you look back at your life story and past patterns around Jupiter in that sign and house so you can apply the insights you glean to your most recent experiences last year.

3. Explore the sign that Jupiter will be moving into next in the upcoming months or year, at the time you are reading this. This can help prepare you to consciously work with the upcoming energy, based on your under-standing of the ways you've experienced it in the past.

4. Explore specific important years or events in your life, and look up where Jupiter was in the cosmos, and how it was interacting with your natal chart and planets that year. Some examples might be when you became a parent, got married or divorced, had a huge career shift, had profound growth in some aspect of your life, or what you remember as your happiest year of your life. To work with a specific year or date, use the Jupiter

Years in the Signs reference table in Appendix C, refer to your ephemeris (see Appendix B), or use an online chart calculation tool to run a transit chart for that specific date to help you identify where Jupiter was in your chart at that time.

5. Look at times in your life when Jupiter by transit in the universe was conjunct a specific planet in your chart, to help you make meaning around how that planet's energy was being magnified and expanded at that time. For instance, with my Moon and Sun conjunct each other in 25 and 27 degrees of Aquarius, I might want to do a worksheet to reflect on what I can learn from each time Jupiter was hanging out in 22-29 degrees of Aquarius every twelve years.

Since I am only providing one template of the My Jupiter Sign and House Cycle Worksheet in this physical book, you will need to make copies to work with, or download the .pdf file (instructions on pg.21) of the worksheet to print or work with on your computer. You can also use the blank journal pages in Appendix E. Find the process that works for you.

My Jupiter Sign and House Cycles Worksheet

Jupiter's Sign by Transit _______________________________

Using Appendix C, record below the year(s) that Jupiter returned to this sign and your age at that return (year in sign - year of my birth + age)

Year ____________________ Age ___________________

Year ____________________ Age ___________________

Year ____________________ Age ___________________

Year ____________________ Age ___________________

Year ____________________ Age ___________________

Keywords and themes of that sign (use Reference Guide to the Signs in Chapter 3)

Referring back to my natal chart, which houses of my chart does this sign occupy? (ex. last part of 4th, 5th house cusp, 1st part of 5th) What are some keywords and themes of those houses? (see chapter 4 Reference Guide to the Houses)

Important memories of myself, people, and events in my life at that time:

What interests was I enthusiastically pursuing, learning, and growing around?

What brought me the greatest joy? What did I feel optimistic, hopeful, and full of possibility about?

What were my dreams and ideals at that time? Did I have a vision or aim for my future? What was it?

Is there something I felt lucky or abundant about?

Was I going to excess or extremes around anything at that age?

What were my core beliefs, philosophies, or spiritual pursuits at that age?

How was I growing in ways specific to the themes of the house(s) Jupiter was moving through in my chart? What was I aspiring towards in that area of my life? What aspirations, faith or prosperity did I experience in that area of my life?

Referring back to my natal chart, what planets, if any, do I have in that sign that Jupiter would come into conjunction with and amplify during this transit? How did that show up in my life? (Refer back to Chapter 5 for keywords and some potential ways that Jupiter-planet conjunction may express).

Optional (intermediate/advanced): What planets do I have in the signs that are trine, square or in opposition to the current Jupiter sign? How did Jupiter's connection with these other planetary energies help or hinder my growth during this transit?

What new awareness have I arrived at through this reflection exercise? What are my takeaways about when Jupiter returns to this sign?

How do I want to apply this new learning as I move forward into who I am becoming and what I intend to accomplish next? Take a look at Chapter 8 for suggested practices to align with the energy of Jupiter in this sign -- it may spark new ideas and goals.

Extra worksheet space

Chapter 7: Outer Planet Transits to My Jupiter

If you've arrived at this chapter, you've already done a lot of introspection about Jupiter's return and transit cycles through your life. In this chapter, you will look at some of the possible ways you might grow and transform when Saturn (an outer "social" planet), and Uranus, Neptune and Pluto (outer "transpersonal" or "collective" planets) in the Universe make contact with your natal Jupiter. These are slower-moving transits that may only occur a handful of times in your entire life, if at all, and when they do, they endure for an extended period of time. That steady energy will color and flavor your experience of personal growth, vision, trust, and prosperity during those years in palpable ways.

Saturn takes approximately 29.5 years to make one complete cycle through the zodiac, spending approximately 2.5 years in a given sign.

Uranus takes approximately 84 years to make one complete cycle through the zodiac, spending approximately 7 years in a given sign.

Neptune takes approximately 160 years to move through the entire zodiac, spending approximately 14 years in a given sign.

Pluto takes approximately 248 years to move through the entire zodiac, spending approximately 12-20 years in a given sign.

Depending on the orb of influence you are considering to be an impactful aspect, the energy of one of these planets being conjunct, trine, square or opposing your natal Jupiter may last from several months to up to five years.

Conjunctions are the most powerful connections and simplest to locate and make sense of. If you live past 90, Saturn will have come into conjunction with your Jupiter a maximum of three times. If you live to at least 84, Uranus will have come into conjunction with your Jupiter at least once. Regardless of how long your lifespan, it is possible that Neptune and Pluto may never come into a conjunction with your Jupiter, or may make this contact once, depending on where those planets are relative to Jupiter in your birth chart.

If you are a complete beginner to astrology, or even if you are more advanced, you may just want to explore the conjunctions. But if you want to go deeper and don't mind the math, you can use your trusty ephemeris (refer to Appendix B) to look up when each of these outer planets was connecting to your natal Jupiter's sign and degree by an aspect other than conjunction (ie. square, trine, opposition).

As a useful resource, here is the reference table copied from Chapter 5, to help you locate which other signs aspect your natal Jupiter's sign.

Reference Table of Aspect Relationships Between Signs

Sign	Trine	Square	Opposition
Aries	Leo, Sagittarius	Cancer, Capricorn	Libra
Taurus	Virgo, Capricorn	Leo, Aquarius	Scorpio
Gemini	Libra, Aquarius	Virgo, Pisces	Sagittarius
Cancer	Scorpio, Pisces	Aries, Libra	Capricorn
Leo	Aries, Sagittarius	Taurus, Scorpio	Aquarius
Virgo	Taurus, Capricorn	Gemini, Sagittarius	Pisces
Libra	Gemini, Aquarius	Cancer, Capricorn	Aries
Scorpio	Cancer, Pisces	Leo, Aquarius	Taurus
Sagittarius	Aries, Leo	Virgo, Pisces	Gemini
Capricorn	Taurus, Virgo	Aries, Libra	Cancer
Aquarius	Gemini, Libra	Scorpio, Taurus	Leo
Pisces	Cancer, Scorpio	Gemini, Sagittarius	Virgo

For example, let's say your natal Jupiter is at 05° of Gemini and you want to identify if and when Saturn formed a transit aspect to your natal Jupiter, and let's say you are working with an orb of +/- 5 degrees:

You will use the ephemeris to identify when Saturn was passing through:

- 0 to 10 degrees of Gemini, forming a conjunction with your Jupiter
- 0-10 degrees of Libra or Aquarius, forming a trine with your Jupiter
- 0-10 degrees of Pisces or Virgo, forming a square with your Jupiter
- and 0-10 degrees of Sagittarius, forming an opposition to your natal Jupiter

Once you know when the outer planet was connecting with your Jupiter, you can use the Outer Planet to Natal Jupiter Worksheet in this chapter, to reflect on what was happening and how you were growing at that time. As always, trust yourself, be patient and compassionate, and allow the new insights to bring you more power and peace in the present.

You can also apply these worksheets to infer what you might expect from an upcoming transit, so that you can consciously prepare for, and work constructively with that energy for your highest good.

A note for advanced astrologers (or for beginners consulting with a professional astrologer): If you have access to the knowledge to do so, you may also want to explore any significant Jupiter-related events by secondary progression and/or solar arc direction. For instance, what is your soul growing and aiming towards when progressed or directed Jupiter is conjunct a planet in your chart, or when a progressed or directed planet is conjunct your natal Jupiter.

Saturn Transits to My Natal Jupiter Worksheet

♃ Jupiter   Sign ——————— Degree ———————

♄ Saturn

Sign	Degrees	Dates	Aspect
———	———	———	———
Sign	Degrees	Dates	Aspect
———	———	———	———
Sign	Degrees	Dates	Aspect
———	———	———	———
Sign	Degrees	Dates	Aspect
———	———	———	———

Saturn -- what I work hard at, take seriously and am committed to, where I apply self-discipline, limits, boundaries, rules, my relationship to my aging and adulthood, what I seek to materialize/manifest/accomplish, legacy, what I am afraid to fail at, mastery, structure, authority, patience, effort, social status, tradition

Saturn transit to natal Jupiter may present like:

- I have an extra dose of seriousness, perseverance, and discipline to work towards accomplishing my vision
- I feel restricted, limited, blocked or stuck around my success or abundance
- I have a big fear of failure or struggle to have faith in my ability to be successful
- I have boundless patience to work steadily towards long-range goals and purpose
- I seek to grow and improve myself through slow, methodical, strategic, long-term effort
- I am creating a plan and structure to manifest my ideals into reality
- My sense of responsibility interferes with my spontaneous joy, adventure or optimism
- I am committed to my spiritual practices, higher learning and truth-seeking
- My practicality and caution hold me back from growing myself through new opportunities and learning

Important memories of myself, people, and events in my life that stand out during this transit time frame:

How did this transit influence my dreams, ideals, sense of higher purpose, faith, or prosperity in my life at that time?

How did this transit influence the pursuits I was growing around? How did it impact my enthusiasm, joy, and optimism?

What have I become aware of through this reflection exercise? What are my takeaways about my soul's growth, purpose, and abundance?

Uranus Transits to My Natal Jupiter Worksheet

♃ Jupiter   Sign _________________   Degree _________________

♅ Uranus

Sign	Degrees	Dates	Aspect
________	________	________	________
Sign	Degrees	Dates	Aspect
________	________	________	________
Sign	Degrees	Dates	Aspect
________	________	________	________
Sign	Degrees	Dates	Aspect
________	________	________	________

Uranus -- my sense of my own uniqueness, how/where I have an urge to change and pursue greater freedom and authenticity, sudden and unexpected events, changes, disruptions and upheavals, flashes of insight, rebellion, non-conformity, eccentricity, future-thinking, humanitarian, technology, progress, innovation

Uranus transit to natal Jupiter may present like:

- I have impulsive urges to change and challenge my traditional ideals, religion or philosophy on life
- I feel irritable or anxious about big changes in my life, and struggle to trust in new possible paths to bring happiness or abundance
- I have sudden, unexpected flashes of vision, inspiration, insight and wisdom
- New, interesting, unconventional, non-conforming people and opportunities show up in my life
- I am attracted to new spiritual practices, new cultures, and international travel
- I have sudden gains or losses, windfalls of success, and lucky prosperity or big disappointments around loss, scarcity and failure
- I may question or explore my sexual or gender identity in a new way
- My rebelliousness or refusal to submit to conventional rules creates an obstacle to my abundance and growth
- I feel unlucky, pessimistic or victimized by sudden unexpected disruptions and upheavals in my life

Important memories of myself, people, and events in my life that stand out during this transit time frame:

How did this transit influence my dreams, ideals, sense of higher purpose, faith, or prosperity in my life at that time?

How did this transit influence the pursuits I was growing around? How did it impact my enthusiasm, joy, and optimism?

What have I become aware of through this reflection exercise? What are my takeaways about my soul's growth, purpose, and abundance?

Neptune Transits to My Natal Jupiter Worksheet

♃ Jupiter   Sign ———————— Degree ————————

♆ Neptune

Sign	Degrees	Dates	Aspect
———	———	———	———
Sign	Degrees	Dates	Aspect
———	———	———	———
Sign	Degrees	Dates	Aspect
———	———	———	———
Sign	Degrees	Dates	Aspect
———	———	———	———

Neptune -- the collective consciousness, spiritual beliefs, connection to Soul, emotional sensitivity and intuition, transcendence, higher consciousness, Oneness, higher power/Source/Divinity/Infinite/God, imagination, fantasy, escape, surrender and faith in the unknown, go with the flow, ego-death, merging with other, co-dependence, confusion, illusion/disillusionment, unconscious, music, movies, alcohol/drugs/psychedelics, video gaming, meditation/ mysticism, yoga

Neptune transit to natal Jupiter may present like:

- I have big aspirations around connecting and merging with Oneness, transcendence and seeking truth through spiritual experience
- I have a big need to escape reality and "doing" to be in a state of flow and "being"
- I can overly idealize and romanticize people or experiences, and can be easily gullible, deceived or disillusioned
- My imagination and fantasy life are on overdrive
- I am a dreamer and feel faithful and trusting in Life or a higher power
- I am growing around my empathy, intuition, clairsentience, or musical ability
- I feel blessed and lucky around my innate purpose in life
- I feel confused and disillusioned about connection to a higher purpose
- I feel cloudy and disoriented, unable to focus clearly on daily life
- My addictions, escapist behavior, or spiritual transcendence practices are at odds with my success and abundance

Important memories of myself, people, and events in my life that stand out during this transit time frame:

How did this transit influence my dreams, ideals, sense of higher purpose, faith, or prosperity in my life at that time?

How did this transit influence the pursuits I was growing around? How did it impact my enthusiasm, joy, and optimism?

What have I become aware of through this reflection exercise? What are my takeaways about my soul's growth, purpose, and abundance?

Pluto Transits to My Natal Jupiter Worksheet

♃ Jupiter   Sign ________________   Degree ________________

♇ Pluto

Sign	Degrees	Dates	Aspect
____	____	____	____
Sign	Degrees	Dates	Aspect
____	____	____	____
Sign	Degrees	Dates	Aspect
____	____	____	____
Sign	Degrees	Dates	Aspect
____	____	____	____

Pluto -- collective crisis and transformation, how I transform and evolve through intensity, power, sex, loss/death/grief/ pain, personal power/powerlessness, abuse/manipulation, where I hit my lowest and rise up again, "dark night of the soul" crisis experiences, rebirth, redemption, resilience in overcoming loss, resurrection, secrecy and control, shadow/ depth psychology, mental health struggles, depression, empowerment and healing, wealth

<u>Pluto transit to natal Jupiter may present like:</u>

- I have powerful transformative experience that challenge my faith, beliefs, and optimism
- Death, loss, power/control, resilience, sex, and/or abuse are big important themes in my life
- I experience deep healing, rebirth, evolution, and empowerment
- I feel unlucky or pessimistic about the painful, dark shadow aspects of myself, others and my experience of the world
- My most profound growth and learning come from challenging losses, death, abuse or grief
- I have ideals and vision around transformational psychology and mental health
- I feel suspicious, secretive, or untrusting of other people's agendas in joint ventures and relationships
- I come into an abundance of money, wealth, inheritance or power

Important memories of myself, people, and events in my life that stand out during this transit time frame:

How did this transit influence my dreams, ideals, sense of higher purpose, faith, or prosperity in my life at that time?

How did this transit influence the pursuits I was growing around? How did it impact my enthusiasm, joy, and optimism?

What have I become aware of through this reflection exercise? What are my takeaways about my soul's growth, purpose, and abundance?

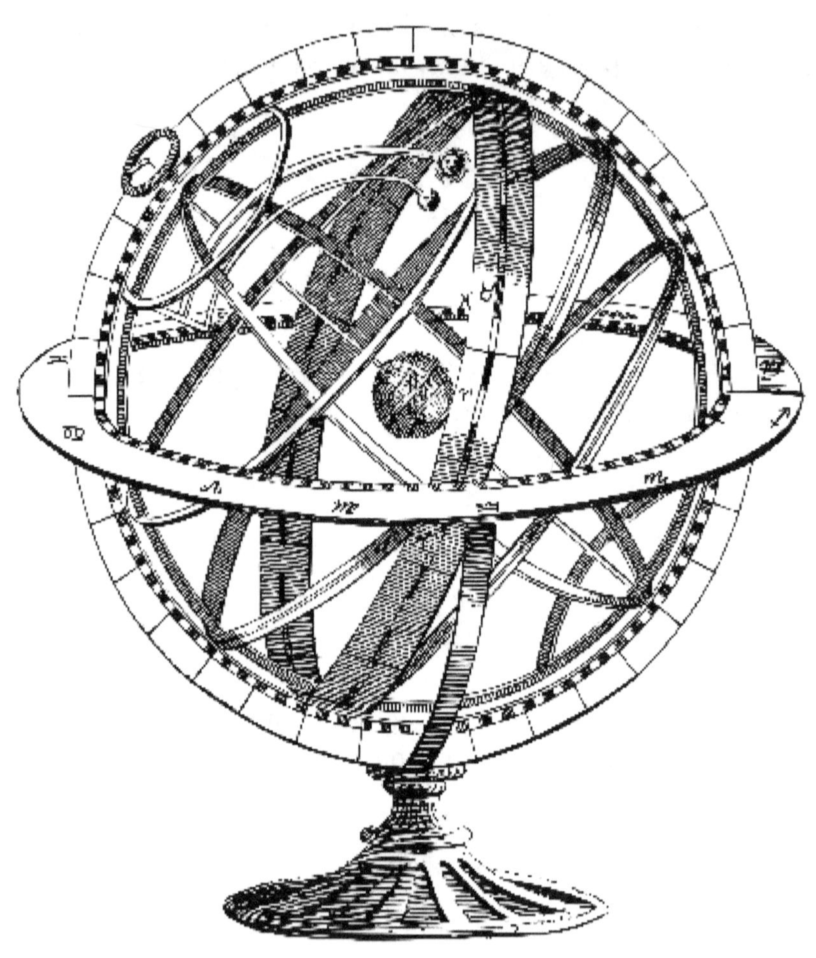

Chapter 8: Practices for Aligning with Jupiter's Potential

Suggested Practices for Jupiter in each sign

Jupiter in Aries Practices
- take new action on your dreams, vision and goals
- learn a martial art (boxing, karate, weaponry)
- engage in strong physical exercise and exertion
- compete at something
- assert yourself with boldness and directness
- engage in qi gong or other vital energy practice
- learn and practice kapalabhati breath of fire kriya
- initiate an independent project
- have a solo travel adventure somewhere new
- prioritize yourself over others
- expand and grow yourself in the area where you have Aries in your chart

Jupiter in Taurus Practices
- luxuriate in comfort
- learn new cooking skills and recipes
- plant a garden
- redecorate your home

- take an art class
- get a fashion and hair makeover
- immerse yourself in the outdoors and Nature
- solidify and realign with your core values
- build up your financial security -- save money, review your budget
- prioritize your physical body and health
- expand and grow yourself in the area where you have Taurus in your chart

Jupiter in Gemini Practices

- learn lots and lots of new things you are curious about
- go back to school for a new course of study or certification
- study a new language
- take music lessons or spend more time playing your instrument
- walk, dance, and move your body
- spend time with friends and social groups
- make new friends, especially with people who can teach you new things
- expand your social media presence, marketing or branding
- teach, write, speak or publish, especially around some wisdom or beliefs you feel spiritually called to shares with others
- take local trips and short excursions
- expand and grow yourself in the area where you have Gemini in your chart

Jupiter in Cancer Practices

- prioritize your self-care and self-love in a big way
- feel your feelings
- spend time near or immersing in natural bodies of water
- spend time with children
- get pregnant, adopt, or birth a child
- enjoy being a homebody and cocooning
- give your living environment some loving care to make it more comfortable
- go on a trip to visit family, or have an adventure with family
- do therapy or healing work around your inner child and family wounds
- care for, nurture or nurse a loved one in need
- engage in developing your intuition and faith
- sort through old photos and memorabilia
- expand and grow yourself in the area where you have Cancer in your chart

Jupiter in Leo Practices

- have more fun, be playful, play games
- creatively express yourself through a project you are passionate about
- take an acting class, expand yourself through theater and entertainment
- start a new romance or flirtation
- boldly step into a new, expansive leadership role
- spend time with children, have children
- get creative around the arts
- practice metta loving-kindness meditation to open

your heart and expand your compassion for all beings including yourself

- sunbathe
- do strength-building, core or fiery bootcamp/ HIIT workouts
- watch superhero movies, be the hero/heroine in your own story or for others
- expand and grow yourself in the area where you have Leo in your chart

Jupiter in Virgo Practices

- start a new nutrition program or dietary plan
- be bold and optimistic about a new exercise and fitness routine
- do a detox or colonic
- declutter and organize your physical living space
- plan and manage a big event
- schedule those doctor appointments and attend to your health
- volunteer your time and service to an organization or cause you care about
- adopt a pet
- practice relinquishing control and letting others make mistakes
- take on a bigger role or promotion in your workplace
- expand and grow yourself in the area where you have Virgo in your chart

Jupiter in Libra Practices
- prioritize your relationships
- enjoy loving up your partner and close friends
- go on an adventure with your partner or close friend
- expand your one-on-one personal and professional connections
- spend time immersing yourself in art, beauty, and nature
- learn new calming practices like yoga or meditation to expand your peacefulness, calm and balance
- get counseling or coaching
- get legal affairs in order, update your will
- get involved in advocacy for a social justice and equality cause
- expand and grow yourself in the area where you have Libra in your chart

Jupiter in Scorpio Practices
- commit to therapy, shadow work, or trauma work
- study psychology, stoicism, CBT or DBT therapy
- delve into mysticism, esoteric studies, or magic
- explore your sexual desires
- learn Tarot, develop your psychic intuition, get a psychic reading
- transform yourself, take back your power
- do research to go deeper into an area of interest
- connect with ancestors and people who have passed over
- update your passwords, change your locks, install a security system
- expand and grow yourself in the area where you have Scorpio in your chart

Jupiter in Sagittarius Practices

- travel internationally
- enroll in a new degree, certification, or higher learning program
- teach a course, publish a book
- give a motivational speech or TED talk
- plan a big adventure
- study philosophy, religion, or ethics
- cultivate optimism and faith in what's possible
- expand your vision, dream bigger, take a risk
- immerse yourself in another culture
- study a new spiritual discipline, find a guru/mentor, become a mentor/teacher
- expand and grow yourself in the area where you have Sagittarius in your chart

Jupiter in Capricorn Practices

- vision and make a real plan around accomplishing a long-range project
- grow into your own sense of adulthood and authority
- expand your work effort, perseverance and self-discipline
- reassess your responsibilities - do they align with your higher purpose and spiritual values?
- honor ancestors, revisit your family history and traditions, learn your genealogy
- ask for a promotion or raise, grow into a bigger professional role
- bring structure and discipline to your aspirations
- release obligations you are no longer committed to
- read about or study history, politics, government,

social issues
- expand and grow yourself in the area where you have Capricorn in your chart

Jupiter in Aquarius Practices

- stop caring what other people might think
- express yourself in a new, bold way
- expand your social networks to include more diverse, unconventional people
- get your LGBTQ+ pride on
- explore your own uniqueness
- break some rules
- take time off of work to feel free, roam, do something unexpected
- engage in community service work to help others
- upgrade your technology
- spend more time alone, detach from the crowd to honor your own needs
- dye your hair
- explore "new age" healing modalities, like energy work, crystals, yoga, breathwork, sound healing, and astrology
- expand and grow yourself in the area where you have Aquarius in your chart

Juptier in Pisces Practices

- trust in your imagination, dreams and visions
- practice meditation, yoga, visualization, prayer and/or journaling
- pay attention to your dreams, start a dream journal, join a dream circle, learn to lucid dream

- develop your empathy, intuition and psychic receptivity
- immerse yourself in music, poetry, film
- take time alone to feel all your feelings and be an introvert
- join a 12 step or other therapeutic healing program to overcome your addictions
- study spiritual philosophies and engage in transcendence practices for awakening consciousness and connecting with Oneness
- swim, float and spend time in or near water
- expand and grow yourself in the area where you have Pisces in your chart

Suggested Practices for Jupiter in any sign

Since Jupiter rules over Thursday, you might set aside some time and space for yourself weekly on a Thursday morning or evening for a dedicated Jupiter-inspired practice. This might include directing energy towards your higher purpose and goals, towards any of the practices suggested above for the sign Jupiter is currently in, or towards any of these Jupiterian practices:

- yoga
- meditation
- visualization
- prayer
- journaling
- studying spiritual/philosophical/wisdom/esoteric texts
- watching movies that inspire you or teach you something new
- reflecting on questions that help you connect with your

higher values and soul purpose
- being in action toward your dreams and ideals
- expressing gratitude for the blessings and abundance you have
- making a list of all the things that fill you with happiness and optimism, and then actively doing things on that list

Jupiterian Coaching Questions

Here are some powerful questions that you can meditate or journal on to bring awareness to what really matters most to you. You might choose to write or doodle your reflection in the empty journal pages provided in Appendix E. You might also have a conversation about any of these questions with a friend, or explore them more deeply with a professional coach.

- If I had more money than I would ever need in my life, and money was no longer a factor in my decision-making, what would I choose to do that feels meaningful and joyful to me?
- If I knew I only had a limited amount of time left to live, what would I change and prioritize in the remaining time I have left?
- If I wasn't already committed to the things I have responsibilities around (job, living situation, relationships, financial obligations, etc...), and had a blank slate to redesign my life, which of these commitments would I still choose? Which would I let go of?
- What are my core values? How am I living in accordance with my core values? How might I more consciously align my life with my core values?

- What did I learn this day/week/month/year about myself, about someone else, about the world, about what's important to me?
- What limiting beliefs do I have that hold me back from pursuing my dream? What unhelpful things am I telling myself? Are those things absolutely true? What else might be true?
- What new opportunity, change or risk might I take if I were brave enough and had faith in my skills, resourcefulness, and wisdom?
- If I could enroll in or audit any class or learning experience, just for the fun of it, what subject or class might I take? What would I enjoy learning?
- If I could work in any dream job, what would it be?
- If I could live in any other place or country than I live now, where would it be and why?

Mantra, Affirmation, Vision Boards and Playlists

There is an Indian tradition of chanting mantras to Guru Brihaspati (Jupiter) to invoke divine blessing, protection, and abundance. You can find recordings of the Jupiter or Guru mantra 'Aum Hreem Kleem Hoom Brihaspataye Namah' on Spotify and YouTube.

You might also create your own powerful affirmation, mantra, or mission statement around your highest ideals, vision, or dreams. Any inspiring quote, phrase, or lyric from the culture or of your own creation can become a powerful tool to draw you back into connection and awareness with the ideals you seek to actualize in your life.

If you are a more visual person, you might create a vision

board with images relating to your soul purpose, growth goals and vision. You might create original art, in any form, that is an expression of your Jupiterian connection.

If you love music, you might create a playlist of songs that connect you to your Jupiterian ideals, aspirations, or soul connection. I had a lot of fun making, listening, and vibing to a "Jupiter in Pisces" playlist when Jupiter was transiting through Pisces in 2021-22. You can find it on my Spotify @Robin Wald Cosmic Wisdom

If you are a musician or composer, you might play or create music that helps you tap into your higher spiritual connection.

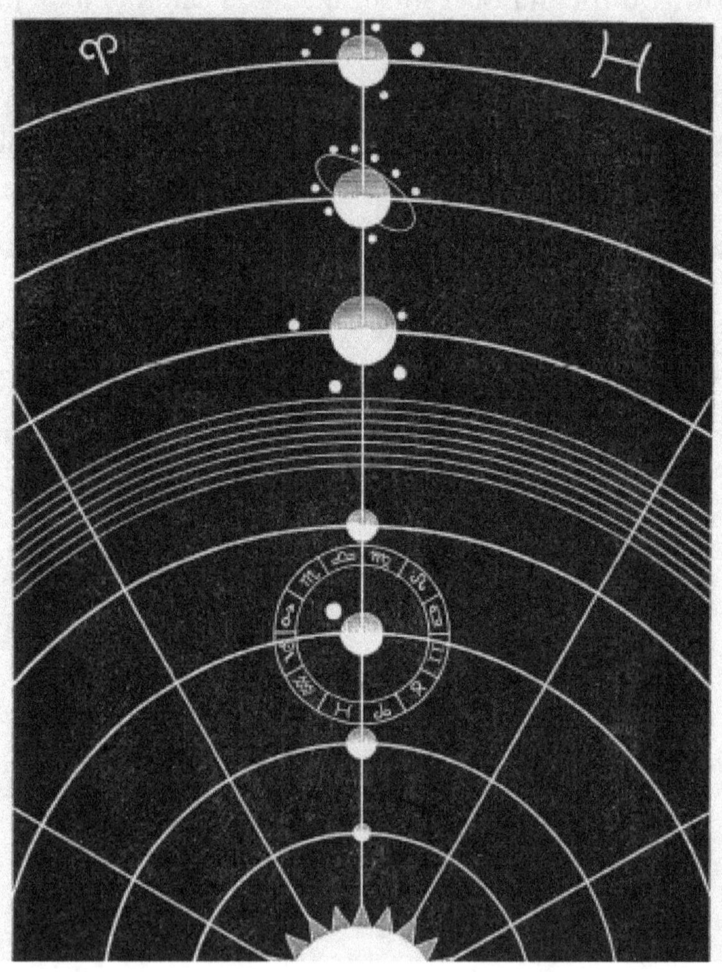

Chapter 9: Tarot for Exploring Jupiterian Themes

Tarot is a method of engaging with archetypal symbols and images to evoke new emotional, intuitive, and memory-based awareness that is a more right-brained pathway for integrating information than through the left-brained rational intellect alone.

"Images are eloquent of themselves. They talk to you. The intellect, when it tries to explicate an image, can never exhaust its meaning, can never exhaust its possibility. Images don't essentially mean anything; they are. Just as you are. And they talk to something within you that is." -- Joseph Campbell

Tarot is an intuitive tool that brings to conscious awareness the wisdom within us through images, symbols, and archetypes. Tarot cards evoke feelings, thoughts, hopes, fears, memories, possibilities. Its images can be akin to dream or fairy-tale images, that bridge us from our left-brained analytical mind to our right-brained intuitive and sensing awareness.

The way I have learned to work with Tarot, with deepest gratitude to my teachers Rachel Pollack and Mary Greer, is that Tarot validates our intuition and inner wisdom. It helps us source from within ourselves potential answers to our questions and concerns, and to open ourselves to hear the messages within our heart and soul. As such, it is not a fortune-telling modality as it is commonly portrayed. The Tarot cards themselves do not predict or determine our future or take away our free will in any way. On the contrary, by mindfully noticing our feelings and thoughts in response to the cards, we actually tap into more free will so we can make empowered choices about how we move forward around our situation.

In the Tarot, Jupiter is associated with the number ten (X) Major Arcana Card -- the Wheel of Fortune. The fact that Jupiter is associated with number 10 is no surprise. Mystically, ten is 1+0, the binary code of all creation, symbolizing all potential and possibility, the individual and the collective, the personal soul and the World Soul, me and the Source/God/One, separate self and no-self merging with All. In Kabbalah, ten sefirot or spheres on the Eytz Chayim "Tree of Life" represent the attributes and interconnectedness of the eternal and earthly realms, of human consciousness and God-consciousness. Jupiter is the planet that speaks to our desire as humans to connect to what is transcendent, spiritual, and divine.

In her book, *Seventy Eight Degrees of Wisdom*, Rachel Pollack refers to the Wheel of Fortune as the "the Mystery of Fate," and "the ever-turning wheel of life." The Wheel of Fortune card's symbols relate to the Jupiterian themes of destiny, purpose, fate, luck, fortune, cycles of change, growth, karma, evolution, enlightenment, faith, and trust in a higher meaning. Different Tarot deck artists use different imagery to convey these themes.

The Rider-Waite-Smith Tarot deck's Wheel of Fortune (pictured below) has symbols from Ezekiel's prophetic vision (*Ezekiel 1:10*) of the heavenly four-faced creatures (*chayot*) that were simultaneously human, lion, ox and eagle, around the spinning wheel containing arrows and the letters of the Tetragrammaton, the unpronounceable four-lettered name of God.

The Light-Seer's Tarot Wheel of Fortune card depicts a woman joyfully balancing in a yogic tree pose atop a tower of spinning wheels, her palms open and receptive to both light and dark, a pair of dice dangling at her heart. Here is a link to the website for Chris-Anne's Light Seer's Tarot (www.lightseerstarot.com), one of my favorite decks, where you can look at all of her card images and explanations.

Jupiter and Tarot Exercises

For this exercise you may choose to work with one or more of the card images provided above, pull the Wheel of Fortune card out of your own Tarot deck(s) if you have that to work with, or search online for other Wheel of Fortune Tarot images you find intriguing that resonate with you.

1. Look carefully at one card. Take in what you see. Is there an image, object, or element of the card that really catches your attention? Describe what you see in detail.

2. How do you feel about this card? Do you feel calm, excited, scared, inspired, happy, angry? Do you feel any physical reaction to the card's images in your body? Do you like this card or dislike it? Why? Describe your physical, emotional, and mental responses to this image.

3. Choose one element, object or being in this card that you want to have a conversation with. Ask it what it wants you to know. Does it have some teaching or offering to share with you? What advice did it offer?

4. Can you imagine yourself in the card, as the main character, or approaching a character or object, or in the landscape? What do you feel or sense about yourself when you place yourself in that archetype energy?

5. It is your choice if or how you use or reject this advice. How might applying this advice help you? What new insight or understanding might be opening up for you just by considering this offering, whether you choose to act on it or not?

6. In what ways do you seek to grow around the themes in this card, especially around higher purpose, faith, ideals, luck, aspirations, and cycles of growth?

Since Jupiter is the planetary ruler of both Sagittarius and Pisces, you might also want to repeat this exercise with the Major Arcana cards of Temperance (Sagittarius) and the Moon (Pisces).

Another helpful exercise would be to repeat this process with the Major Arcana card specifically associated with your natal Jupiter's sign. For instance, since I have Jupiter in Libra, I would look at the Justice card from one or several different Tarot decks. I would notice what the Justice card evokes for me, what I feel and think in response to it, how the archetype of the card resonates with me. I would consider how I am aspiring to learn and grow around the themes in that card. What do the images in the Justice card bring up for me about my ideals, aspirations, and connection to a higher truth or purpose?

Each time Jupiter transits into a new sign, you might have a conversation with the Major Arcana card associated with that sign, as a way of connecting with the energy of that sign. As a meditative exercise, you might be surprised by what your intuitive heart and mind reveal to you about your hopeful joy around how Jupiter might expand you in a new way relating to that Tarot card's archetypal wisdom.

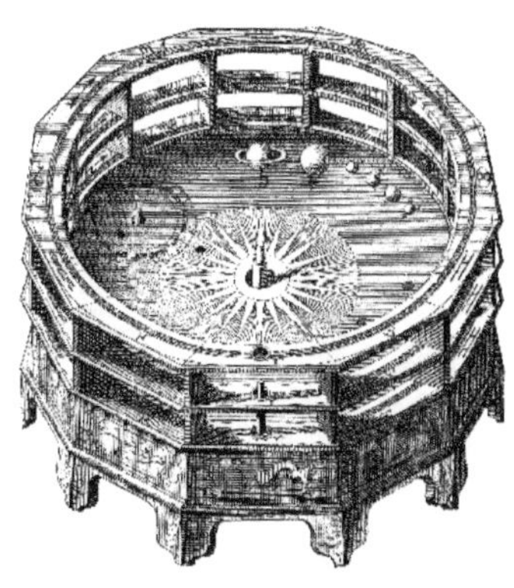

Major Arcana & Zodiac Relationships	
Aries	Emperor
Taurus	Hierophant
Gemini	Lovers
Cancer	Chariot
Leo	Strength
Virgo	Hermit
Libra	Justice
Scorpio	Death
Sagittarius	Temperance
Capricorn	Devil
Acquarius	Star
Pisces	Moon

XIV
TEMPERANCE.

Acknowledgements

This book would not have been possible without all the love, support, and encouragement I've received from so many special people. First and foremost, a deep bow of gratitude to Dominique Nieves, for being my book coach, consultant, editor, designer and all-around writing and publishing guru. This book would not exist in the world if not for your expertise and guidance.

Thank you to my parents, grandparents, and siblings who were my earliest and most impactful teachers. I hit the jackpot being born into our family. Thank you to Maya, Aaron, and Eli -- parenting you into adulthood has been my greatest journey, joy, and legacy. I am immensely proud of each of you for bravely pursuing your unique path and purpose in life.

Thank you to all my students, astrology clients, and coaching clients for trusting me to be your teacher, guide, partner, mentor, cheerleader, and friend. Your growth and becoming is entwined with my own.

Thank you to all my teachers, including friends, partners, students, colleagues, spiritual mentors, and authors who challenged me to grow and expand my curiosity, spirituality, self-awareness, and skillfulness. I am especially grateful to my teachers at Bialik School, Columbia University, Satsang and Sage Yoga, Thich Nhat Hanh, Coach Training World, and the brilliant and soulful women of Bet Torah.

Thank you to Diane Wiener, my childhood friend, for

first introducing me to astrology, to Leda Blumberg, the first professional astrologer I ever consulted with who ignited my desire to study astrology, and to Lucy Gordon, my astrology study partner, for the hundreds of hours we pored over charts sharing insights.

I am grateful to Life, the Mystery, Source, Infinite, Ein Sof, Shechinah, Cosmos, One, for creating, sustaining, and blessing me to arrive at this moment.

Lastly, thank you, dear reader. I hope this book helped you in some way.

About The Author

Robin Wald, ICF-PCC, MS, RYT is a professional consulting astrologer, an internationally certified professional coach, a yoga and meditation instructor, an intuitive Tarot reader, and a passionate student and teacher of spiritual wisdom. Through her business, Cosmic Wisdom Coaching, Robin is grateful and honored to do powerful one-on-on transformational work with adult and young adult clients, to support their self-exploration, growth, wellness, joy and success. Upcoming titles she is authoring in this Astrology Coaching Workbook series include *My Saturn for Accomplishment and Mastery* (late 2023) and *My Chiron for Healing and Wisdom* (2024). You can find out more and subscribe to Robin's free monthly cosmic wisdom teaching and video, at www.robinwald.com and on YouTube @robinwaldcosmicwisdom.

Appendix A -- Bibliography References

Arroyo, Stephen. *Chart Interpretation Handbook: Guidelines for Understanding the Essentials of the Birth Chart.* CRCS Publications, 1989.

Arroyo, Stephen. *Exploring Jupiter: The Astrological Key to Progress, Prosperity & Potential.* CRCS Publications, 1996.

Arroyo, Stephen. *Astrology, Psychology and the Four Elements.* CRCS Publications, 1975.

Arroyo, Stephen. *Relationships and Life Cycles: Modern Dimensions of Astrology.* CRCS Publications, 1979.

Cunningham, Donna. *How to Read Your Astrological Chart.* Weiser Books, 1999.

Fowks, Lauran and Sellon, Lynn. *Simply Math: A Comprehensive Guide to Easy and Accurate Chart Calculation.* Twelfth House Press, 2005.

Hand, Robert. *Horoscope Symbols.* Whitford Press, 1981.

Hand, Robert. *Planets in Transit: Life Cycles for Living.* Whitford Press, 2001.

Huber, Bruno and Louise and Huber, Michael-Alexander. *Aspect Pattern Astrology.* HopeWell, 2019.

Meyers, Eric. T*he Astrology of Awakening, Volume 1: Eclipse of the Ego.* Astrology Sight Publishing, 2012.

Michelsen, Neil. *The American Ephemeris for the 20th Century 1900 to 2000 at Midnight, Revised Fifth Edition.* ACS Publications. 1995.

Michelsen, Neil. *The American Ephemeris for 21st Century 2000 to 2050 at Midnight, Expanded Second Edition.* ACS Publications.1997.

Pelletier, Robert. *Planets in Aspect: Understanding Your Inner Dynamics.* Whitford Press, 1974.

Ruperti, Alexander. C*ycles of Becoming: The Planetary Pattern of Growth.* Earthwalk School of Astrology, 2005.

Sasson, Gahl Eden. *Cosmic Navigator.* Weiser Books, 2008.

Tarnas, Richard. *An Introduction to Archetypal Astrology.* WordPress. *https://cosmosandpsyche.files.wordpress. com/2013/05/introductiontoastrology1.pdf*

Tarnas, Richard. *Cosmos and Psyche.* Plume Books, 2007.

Tompkins, Sue. *Aspects in Astrology: A Guide to Understanding Planetary Relationships in the Horoscope.* Destiny Books, 2002.

Appendix B -- How to Use an Ephemeris, and a Look at Aspect Patterns

How to Use an Ephemeris

An ephemeris is a listing of all planets' positions in the zodiac on any given day in the past, present, or future. It is used by astrologers to hand-calculate a person's birth chart, using math to extrapolate the exact degrees and minutes of each planet to the exact location in the world (longitude and latitude) and time (relative to Greenwich Mean Time) that an individual was born on this Earth. It is also used to identify planetary transits and cycles to a person's birth chart.

The way you might want or need to use an ephemeris for the purpose of this book is to explore your Jupiter cycles and transits (Chapters 6 and 7).

The American Ephemeris, 20th century and 21st century editions by Neil Michelsen are the print book ephemerides I keep handy for use. I recommend you borrow them from a library or purchase them if you want to invest in owning these for future reference. Or you can consult these free online ephemerides:

Astrodienst ephemeris

Astro-Seek ephemeris

Let's walk through step-by-step examples together for how you would use the ephemeris.

1. To pinpoint your Jupiter returns' most powerful conjunction dates

Jupiter in my birth chart is at 4°♎55" (Retrograde). Since

I was born in Feb 1969, and Jupiter returns to the same degree approximately every 12 years, I will expect to find Jupiter to be somewhere in the proximity of 4-5 degrees of Libra when I am 12 in 1981 (1969+12=1981), 24 in 1993 (1969+24=1993), 36 in 2005, 48 in 2017, etc... If I want to find out when my next Jupiter return will be, I can follow the math to see that my next return will be somewhere around 2029 (1969+60=2029).

If I am doing the My Jupiter Returns Worksheet in Chapter 6 and want to reflect back on my most recent Jupiter return at around age 48, I will open my ephemeris to February 2017 as a starting point. If I am using the online ephemeris, I will click on the link to 2017 and look at the February table.

If I consider my Jupiter return to be when transiting Jupiter is loosely within an aspect orb of +/- 3 degrees of my natal 4 (almost 5) degree Libra, I will search the ephemeris tables to find when Jupiter was between 1 to 8 degrees of Libra.

In the ephemeris on February 1, 2017, I scan across to the Jupiter symbol and check the degree and sign Jupiter was occupying on that date. I see that Jupiter was at 23 degrees 5.8 minutes of Libra.

Since I am looking for when Jupiter was in 1-8 degrees of Libra, I backtrack through the prior months of the ephemeris (Jan 2017, Dec 2016, Nov 2016, etc.) until I locate when Jupiter first entered 1 degree, which was on September 15, 2016. Now I scan forward through the dates to see when Jupiter was last at 8 degrees of Libra, which was on October 21, 2016.

I now know that the most potent timing of my 4th Jupiter return was Sep 15-Oct 21, 2016. I will record that date range on my worksheet for my 4th Jupiter return, and reflect on any specific people, events or other memories that stand out for me during those specific dates.

A note about planets in retrograde: When a planet is moving retrograde (apparently backtracking through the zodiac from our Earthly perspective), the ephemeris indicates this by shading the box on that date. There will be an R placed at the date when the retrograde initiates, and again at the top of the column for a new month if the planet is still in retrograde. If you come across a Jupiter retrograde at the degrees you are looking for, make sure to look through previous and future months around that date, since Jupiter may make two or three separate passes, forward then backwards then forward again, over your natal Jupiter during that return.

2. To identify the sign and degree Jupiter was in on a given day or time of a significant life event that you want to explore deeper

This is super-easy. Say you got married on June 11, 2000. You just open your ephemeris to that date and see where Jupiter was by degree and sign in the universe on that date. Using that information, you can see what house that Jupiter transit was happening in and what planets it was aspecting in your chart. You can then refer back to the "My Jupiter Sign and House Worksheet" in Chapter 6 to create new insights about how Jupiter was expanding you and bringing you abundance and happiness at that moment in your life.

3. To identify when Saturn, Uranus, Neptune or Pluto

were or will be in aspect to your natal Jupiter
(for Chapter 7 work with outer and transpersonal
planet transits)

One of the quickest ways to find out when any of these planets was last in a given sign (either your Jupiter's natal sign, or a sign square, opposing or trine) is to just Google it, as a starting point. Once you have the year ranges, you can then use your ephemeris to look up those years and hone in on the degrees you are looking at that would have been in aspect to your natal Jupiter.

For instance, say I want to identify the times in my life that Saturn was conjunct my natal Jupiter in Libra. When I search online for "Saturn in Libra years" what shows up is "Apr 6, 1924 to Sep 13, 1924. Nov 20, 1950 to Mar 7, 1951. Aug 13, 1951 to Oct 22, 1953. Sep 21, 1980 to Nov 29, 1982, Oct 29, 2009 to Apr 7, 2010, Jul 21, 2010 to Oct 5, 2012."

Based on when I've been alive, I now know that Saturn was in Libra twice in my life, between Sept 1980 and Nov 1982, and again between Oct 2009 and Oct 2012. Referencing my ephemeris, using Sept 1980 as a starting point, I find that Saturn was between 1-8 degrees of Libra from Sept 31-Dec 20, 1980, then again (because Saturn retrograded) from Feb 18 - Sept 4, 1981. I was 11 and 12 years old at that time. Wow! I just created brand new awareness that Saturn was conjunct my Jupiter during my very first Jupiter return! I know this because I was 12 - a Jupiter return year - and can easily confirm it in the ephemeris if I look in the Jupiter column for the 1980-1 timeframe, showing Jupiter was in 1-8 degrees of Libra from June to August of 1981. I will sit with this new information, and process through my new awareness using the Saturn Transits to My Natal Jupiter Worksheet in Chapter 7. I can repeat this exercise for the second Saturn-Jupiter conjunction, and for Uranus, Neptune and Pluto aspects to my Jupiter as well.

A Look at Aspect Patterns

Stellium (will look like three or more planets and points all grouped together in the same sign or house) -- this creates a strong concentration of energy and emphasis on that sign or house.

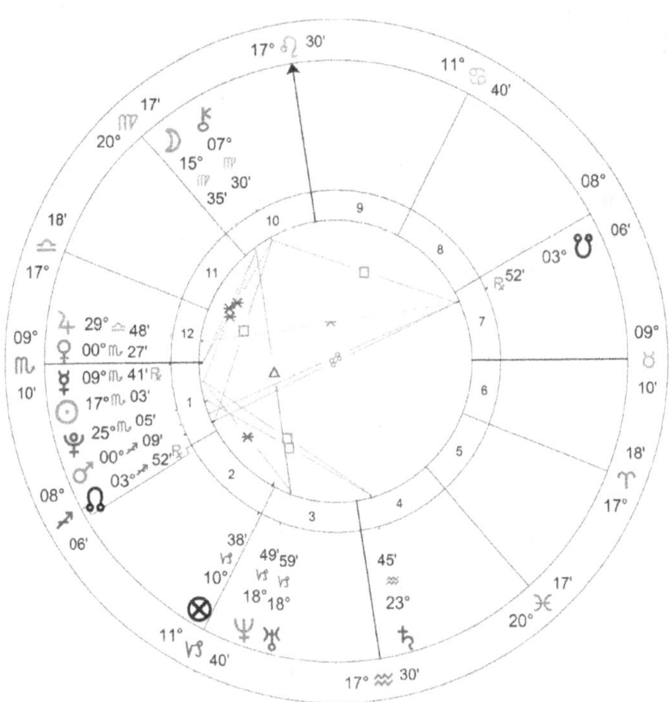

Sample chart of a Scorpio stellium (Venus, Ascendant, Mercury, Sun, Pluto) and a 1st house stellium (Mercury, Sun, Pluto, Mars, North Node)

Another example is my natal chart (in Chapter 2) which has 1st house and 7th house stelliums.

Grand Trine (will look like a blue equilateral triangle in your chart with planets 120-120-120 apart from each other) -- this creates a natural ease, blessing and attunement to the element the planets are in (fire, earth, air, water) in each of its modalities (cardinal, fixed and mutable). A Grand Trine is a blessing and bestows special talents. like a super-power, in that element. The flip side is that a person with a grand trine may become overly reliant on one elemental resource to the exclusion of building their resourcefulness in others. Some astrologers caution that this configuration may lead to a laziness or taking for granted that resource, or an inability to understand or practically access different perspectives.

Grand Cross (will look like a red square with two 180 oppositions and four 90-degree squares, usually in the same mode of energy -- cardinal, fixed or mutable) -- this creates a lot of tension and stress that yearns to be resolved and integrated. A Grand Cross can be very challenging, especially earlier in life, but may prove to be highly motivating, creative, and transformative. It also attunes you strongly to its mode quality -- having a lot of cardinal energy to initiate and begin things, fixed energy to persist and stubbornly stick with things, or mutable energy to let go, release and adapt.

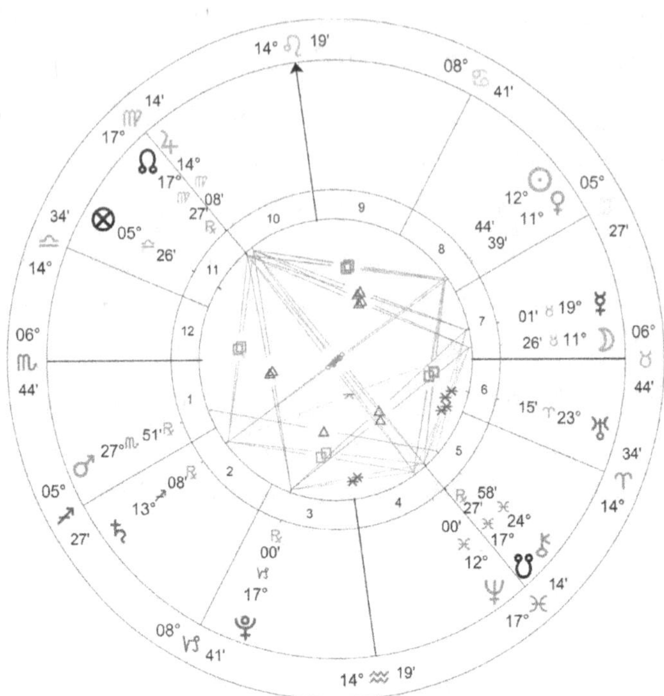

Sample chart containing both a Grand Trine in Earth (Jupiter and North Node in Virgo trine Pluto in Capricorn trine Moon and Mercury in Taurus) and a mutable Grand Cross (Jupiter and North Node in Virgo squaring Saturn in Sagittarius squaring Neptune and South Node in Pisces squaring Sun and Venus in Gemini, with the oppositions between the Virgo-Pisces and Gemini-Sagittarius planets).

T - Square (will look like a red right triangle with two planets 180 degrees opposite each other, and a third focal planet(s) at a 90 degree square from both of those opposing planets) -- this is similar to but slightly less stressful than the grand cross, indicating tensions that need to be creatively resolved and integrated. Like the base of a see-saw, the planet at the fulcrum between the two opposing planets can be the key to integrating and balancing the different energies that are at odds with each other. Points in a T-square generally occupy the same modal quality (cardinal, fixed or mutable).

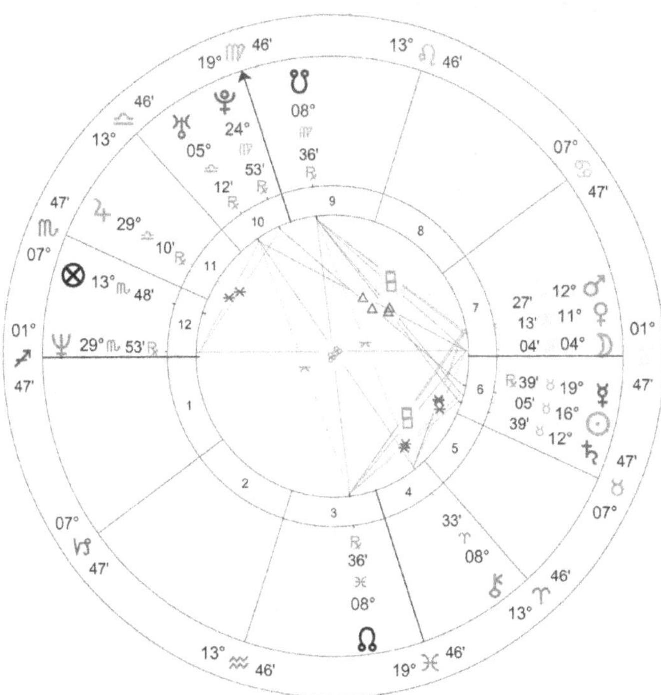

A sample chart containing a mutable T-square with the Moon, Venus and Mars in Gemini squaring the North Node in Pisces and South Node in Virgo which oppose each other.

Yod (will look like two green lines emanating from a single point and opening out at 150-degree quincunx to two other planets that are blue sextile 60 degrees from each other) -- this configuration is known as the "finger of god" and points you towards a special mission or task to understand in this lifetime, that may require hard lessons and sacrifice. The planet at the "apex" or eye of the telescope is

199

the key to help you focus, connect, and beneficially grow and evolve between the energies of the two sextile planets.

An example of a yod can be found in my natal chart in Chapter 2, with Pluto in Virgo quincunx the Sun and Moon in Aquarius, and quincunx Saturn in Aries, with Sun/Moon and Saturn sextile each other.

There are other significant aspect patterns, such as a kite, a mystics rectangle, a lesser triangle, a Star of David, and others. For a deeper dive into the meanings of aspect patterns, I recommend Huber's book, *Aspect Pattern Astrology*, listed in Appendix A

Appendix C -- Jupiter Years in the Signs Reference Tables

Jupiter in Aries

Jun 7 - Sep 11, 1927, Jan 24 - June 4, 1928

May 13, 1939 - Oct 30, 1939, Dec 21, 1939- May 16, 1940

Apr 22, 1951 - Apr 28, 1952

Apr 5, 1962 - Apr 13, 1964

Mar 18, 1975 - Mar 27, 1976

Mar 2, 1987 - Mar 8, 1988

Feb 12 - Jun 28, 1999, Oc 23, 1999 - Feb 14, 2000

Jun 6 - Sep 9, 2010, Jan 22 - Jun 4, 2011

May 10 - Oct 28, 2022, Dec 20, 2022 - May 16, 2023

Jupiter in Taurus

June 5, 1928 - Jun 12, 1929

May 17, 1940 - May 26, 1941

Apr 28, 1952 - May 9, 1953

Apr 13, 1964 - Apr 23, 1965

Mar 27 - Aug 23, 1976, Oct 17, 1976 - Apr 4, 1977

Mar 11 - Jul 21, 1988, Dec 1, 1988 - Mar 11, 1989

Jun 28 - Oct 23, 1999, Feb 14 - Jun 30, 2000

Jun 4, 2011 - Jun 11, 2012

May 16, 2023 - May 25, 2024

Jupiter in Gemini

Jun 13, 1929 - Jun 26, 1930

May 26, 1941 - Jun 10, 1942

May 9, 1953 - May 24, 1954

Apr 23, 1965 - Sep 21, 1965, Nov 17, 1965 - May 6, 1966

Aug 24 - Oct 16, 1976, Apr 4 - Aug 20, 1977, Dec 31 1977-
Apr 12, 1978

Jul 21 - Dec 1, 1988, Mar 11 - Jul 30, 1989

Jun 30, 2000 - Jul 12, 2001

Jun 11, 2012 - Jun 25, 2013

May 25, 2024 - Jun 9, 2025

Jupiter in Cancer

Jun 27, 1930 - Jul 17, 1931

Jun 11, 1942 - Jun 30, 1943

May 24, 1954 - Jun 13, 1955

Sep 21 - Nov 17, 1965, May 6 - Sep 27, 1966, Jan 17 -
May 23, 1967

Aug 21 - Dec 30, 1977, Apr 13 - Sep 5, 1978, Mar 1 -
Apr 20, 1979

Jul 30, 1989 - Aug 18, 1990

July 12, 2001 - Aug 1, 2002

Jun 25, 2013 - Jul 16, 2014

Jun 9, 2025 - Jun 30, 2026

Jupiter in Leo

Jul 17, 1931 - Aug 11, 1932

Jul 1, 1943 - Jul 26, 1944

Jun 13, 1955 - Nov 17, 1955, Jan 18 - Jul 7, 1956

Sep 28, 1966 - Jan 16, 1967, May 24 - Oct 19, 1967, Feb 28 -
Jun 15, 1968

Sep 5, 1978 - Feb 28, 1979, Apr 20 - Sep 29, 1979

Aug 18, 1990 - Sep 12, 1991

Aug 1, 2002 - Aug 27, 2003

Jul 16, 2014 - Aug 11, 2015

Jun 30, 2026 - Jul 26, 2027

Jupiter in Virgo

Jul 12, 1932 - Sep 10, 1933

Jul 27, 1944 - Aug 25, 1945

Nov 17, 1955 - Jan 18, 1956, Jul 8 - Dec 13, 1956, Feb 20
- Aug 7, 1957

Oct 20, 1967 - Feb 27, 1968, Jun 16 - Nov 15, 1968, Mar 31 -
Jul 15, 1969

Sep 29, 1979 - Oct 27, 1980

Sept 12, 1991 - Oct 10, 1992

Aug 27, 2003 - Sep 24, 2004

Aug 11, 2015 - Sep 9, 2016

Jul 26, 2027 - Aug 24, 2028

Jupiter in Libra

Jul 11, 1933 - Oct 11, 1934

Aug 26, 1945 - Sep 25, 1946,

Dec 14, 1956- Feb 19, 1957, Aug 8 - 1957 - Jan 13, 1958, Mar
21 - Sep 7, 1958

Nov 16, 1968 - Mar 30, 1969, Jul 16 - Dec 17, 1969, May 1,
1970 - Aug 15, 1970

Oct 27, 1980 - Nov 27, 1981

Oct 10, 1992 - Nov 10, 1993

Sep 24, 2004 - Oct 25, 2005

Sep 9, 2016 - Oct 10, 2017

Aug 24, 2028 - Sep 24, 2029

Jupiter in Scorpio

Oct 12, 1934 - Nov 9, 1935

Sep 26, 1946 - Oct 24, 1947

Jan 14 - Mar 20, 1958, Sep 8, 1958 - Feb 10, 1959, Apr 25
- Oct 5, 1959

Dec 17, 1969 - Apr 30, 1970, Aug 16, 1970 - Jan 14, 1971, Jun
6 - Sep 11, 1971

Nov 27, 1981 - Dec 26, 1982

Nov 10, 1993 - Dec 9, 1994

Oct 25, 2005 - Nov 24, 2006

Oct 10, 2017 - Nov 8, 2018

Sep 24, 2029 - Oct 22, 2030

Jupiter in Sagittarius

Nov 10, 1935- Dec 2, 1936

Oct 25, 1947 - Nov 15, 1948

Feb 11 - Apr 24, 1959, Oct 6, 1959 - Mar 1, 1960, Jun 11 -
Oct 26, 1960

Jan 15 - Jun 5, 1971, Sep 12, 1971 - Feb 6, 1972, Jul 25 -
Sep 25, 1972

Dec 26, 1982 - Jan 19, 1984

Dec 9, 1994 - Jan 3, 1996

Nov 24, 2006 - Dec 18, 2007

Nov 8, 2018 - Dec 2, 2019

Oct 22, 2030 - Nov 15, 2031

Jupiter in Capricorn

Dec 3, 1936 - Dec 20, 1937

Nov 16, 1948 - Apr 12, 1949, Jun 28 - Nov 30, 1949

Mar 1 - Jun 10, 1960, Oct 27, 1960 - Mar 15, 1961, Aug 13 - Nov 4, 1961

Feb 6 - Jul 24, 1972, Sep 26, 1972 - Feb 23, 1973

Jan 19, 1984 - Feb 6, 1985

Jan 3 1996 - Jan 21, 1997

Dec 18, 2007 - Jan 5, 2009

Dec 2, 2019 - Dec 19, 2020

Nov 15, 2031 - Apr 12, 2032, Jun 26 - Nov 30, 2032

Jupiter in Aquarius

Dec 21, 1937 - Dec 29, 1938

Apr 12 - Jun 27, 1949, Dec 1, 1949 - Apr 15, 1950, Sep 16 - Dec 1, 1950

Mar 16, 1961 - Aug 12, 1961, Nov 5, 1961 - Mar 25, 1962

Feb 24, 1973 - Mar 8, 1974

Feb 6, 1985 - Feb 20, 1986

Jan 21, 1997 - Feb 4, 1998

Jan 5, 2009 - Jan 18, 2010

Dec 19, 2020 - May 13, 2021, Jul 28 - Dec 28, 2021

Apr 12, 2032 - Jun 26, 2032, Nov 30, 2032 - Apr 14, 2033, Sep 12 - Dec 1, 2033

Jupiter in Pisces

Sept 12, 1927 - Jan 23, 1928

Dec 30, 1938- May 12, 1939, Oct 31 - Dec 20, 1939

Apr 16 -Sep 15, 1950, Dec 2, 1950 - Apr 21, 1951

Mar 26, 1962 - Apr 4, 1962

Mar 8, 1974 - Mar 18, 1975

Feb 20, 1986 - Mar 2, 1987

Feb 4, 1998 - Feb 13, 1999

Jan 18 - Jun 6, 2010, Sep 9, 2010- Jan 22, 2011

May 13 - Jul 27, 2021, Dec 28, 2021 - May 9, 2022, Oct 28, 2022 - Dec 19, 2022

Apr 14 - Sep 12, 2033, Dec 1, 2033 - Apr 21, 2034

Appendix D -- Sample Worksheets

My Natal Jupiter Worksheet

My natal Jupiter is in the sign of ___Libra___

My natal Jupiter's degree and minutes is ___04° 55'___

My natal Jupiter is in the ___7th___ house
(accurate house placement is dependant on having an accurate birth time)

My natal Jupiter is Direct / Retrograde (circle which applies)

My natal Jupiter is connected to these planets/points by aspect (see Chapter 5)

Planet/Point	Aspect (conjunction, sextile, trine, square, opposition, inconjunct)
Uranus ♅	conjunction
South Node ☋	conjunction
North Node ☊	opposition
Chiron ⚷	opposition
Mercury ☿	sextile

Is my natal Jupiter part of a special aspect pattern (stellium, grand trine, T-square, grand cross, Yod, mystics rectangle? (see appendix B for more on this)
___Libra stellium with Jupiter/Uranus/S. Node___

My Jupiter - Uranus Aspect Worksheet

♃ Jupiter   sign _Libra_   degrees _4°55'_   house _7th_

♅ Uranus   sign _Libra_   degrees _3°19'_   house _7th_

Jupiter-Uranus aspect _Conjunction_

Uranus -- my sense of my own uniqueness, how/where I break the rules and seek freedom and authenticity, sudden unexpected changes, disruptions and upheavals, flashes of insight, instability, rebellion, non-conformity, eccentricity, futuristic-minded, humanitarianism, technology, progress, innovation

Jupiter- Uranus aspects may present like:

✓ I have a big need for freedom, individuality, and non-conformity   *especially to be my own self + have my own thoughts*

✓ I have sudden, unexpected flashes of vision, inspiration, insight and wisdom

✓ I have many unique, interesting, unconventional beliefs and alternative ideas or spiritual practices   *so many unique and different friends, students, clients of all ages, genders, races*

✓ I proudly identify as LGBTQ, non-binary, and don't conform to heteronormative ideas around sexual and gender identity or expression   *proud ally, so many LGBTQ loved ones*

✓ I grow and learn through sudden, unexpected changes of good or bad fortune in my life

✓ I am idealistic and optimistic for the future of humanity, innovation and social   *✓ teenagers*   advances, or I struggle with pessimism about humanity and the future

✓ I have a big need to travel and experience new places, cultures, and people   *developed this in later adulthood*

✓ I struggle with faith that change will be positive, beneficial or help me align with my purpose and success   *yes, at certain times in my life*   *resistant to change*

~ My rebelliousness or refusal to submit to conventional rules creates an obstacle to my abundance and growth   *unsure, I think my refusal to "obey" without questioning has supported my success*   *non-conventional career path*

~ I feel unlucky, pessimistic or victimized by sudden unexpected disruptions and upheavals in my life   *yes, on occasion, but have also felt so lucky + blessed to be in the right place at the right time to experience something unexpectedly fortunate*

Reflections on how I have experienced my Jupiter-Uranus aspect:

As a younger child, I felt different, shy, like I didn't fit in or belong, or think/act like everyone else.

I was always kind, considerate, thinking about what others want + need, and peace-keeping in relationship. I was more of a giver than a taker, which is still true, but more in balanced as I've grown + learned about fairness in relationship.

I always seek to be my authentic self, to express my own ideas, to trust + value my own insight + unique perspective.

I definitely am a motivated, inspired learner + always curious about out-of-the box, unusual, "new age" type esoteric pursuits.

"Uranian"
"Aquarian"

Studied engineering - civil -
conjunct / Libra / 7th

very
Aquarian
Libra / 7th

Any other reflections, specific to the nature of the aspect, signs and houses?

(Note: as an outer trans-personal planet, everyone born within several years of you has Uranus in the same sign. Uranus' house placement is more personal to where in your chart/life you will experience Uranian themes, and how its relationship with Jupiter supports your growth and faith around those themes.)

I definitely have an abundance of relationships - family, siblings, nieces/nephews, friends, students, peers, study groups, community, clients. I love to be in relationship with all different people. I grow and learn from relationships and diverse people + opinions.

I have a strong sense of joy and connection on a Soul/faith level about being in harmonious relationship with others that is fair, equal, balanced, sharing, cooperative.

How might I consciously apply and leverage my Jupiter/Uranus potential as I move forward towards my dreams, purpose and goals?

I am especially faithful in my ability to connect with others from a place of objectivity, listening, counseling, coaching, partnership, advocacy.

I aim / aspire to continue to grow + learn around these skills to support my professional services and success, and my own spiritual contentment and growth.

My Jupiter - Chiron Aspect Worksheet

♃ Jupiter   sign _Libra_   degrees _4°55'_   house _7th_

⚷ Chiron   sign _Aries_   degrees _0°45'_   house _1st_

Jupiter-Chiron aspect _opposition_

Chiron - the "wounded healer," where I have an early life/childhood wound or feel inadequate/insecure/not enough, emotional wounds or physical health issues I struggle with at intervals, where I have healing work to do in order to fully love and accept myself as an integrated whole, where I become a healer/mentor/guide to others through my own experience of self-healing and integration

<u>Jupiter-Chiron aspects may present like:</u>

✓ I have a strong sense of soul calling and purpose around being a teacher, healer or mentor

✓ I am faithful, trusting and optimistic about the potential to heal wounds and attain wholeness and integration

✓ I feel lucky or <u>blessed</u> around my health   *gratitude for health/strength/function, don't take for granted*

✓ I have a big sense of inadequacy, insecurity, or not being good <u>enough</u> *as a child + was insecure, fearful, very shy and lacking*

✓ I feel challenged or unlucky about my health, or victimized by chronic or serious *confidence* bouts of illness *"sickly" as a child + injury/illness prone; health + immune issues throughout life, chronic pain*

✓ I have limiting beliefs about my worth or ability to receive abundance and prosperity *outgrew this, finally, as an adult, especially at and since Chiron return 49+*

✓ I seek spiritual meaning and adopt an expansive growth-mindset to heal myself and contribute to others' healing

✓ I have aspirations around travel, experiencing new places and cultures, as a way to heal my connection to my own soul, to others and to my higher purpose

✓ I grow and expand myself through seeking mentorship or <u>becoming a mentor</u> *esp. to teens, yes, both clients*

Reflections on how I have experienced my Jupiter-Chiron aspect:

It has been naturally easier for me to lean into relationships, allow others to be assertive, directive, decisive versus stand in my own will + authority. I have often drawn in relationships as a mirror to show me what it looks like to be ambitious, strong-willed, selfish — this hasn't always been easy + has triggered wounds for me, but has also led to my growth + healing.

I definitely have aspirations + sense of soul purpose and ideals around healing myself + being a support for others' healing. I have been in healing professions — nutrition, yoga, meditation, spiritual counseling, coaching.

Any other reflections, specific to the nature of the aspect, signs and houses? opposition / Libra 0—0 Aries / 7th 0—0 1st

The self (Aries/1st h.) Chiron wound in relation to others (Libra/7th) is such a big theme in my life. I have often sacrificed my own needs/goals/will to keep others/relationships secure and happy. I am more naturally inclined to elevate + compromise for the relationship and others — Jupiter in Libra/7th — than to take care of my own needs. I have done so much healing, growing around this, and developing strong sense of self, autonomy, personal will.

How might I consciously apply and leverage my Jupiter/Chiron potential as I move forward towards my dreams, purpose and goals?

I am a mentor/support for others around healing/valuing their sense of self and self-care. The more I heal + integrate around Aries/1st house Chiron themes, especially as a reflection and mirror for my Jupiter soul purpose around relational counseling/coaching/teaching, the greater service I can be for others as a support + role model.

My Jupiter For Personal Growth and Purpose

My Jupiter Return(s) Worksheet

My Natal Jupiter Sign and Degrees _____ 4° 55' Libra_____

Using Appendix C, record below the year(s) that Jupiter returned to your natal Jupiter sign, and your age at that return

(year in sign - year of my birth = age at return)

Year/Date range Jupiter returned to my natal sign: age
  ① Oct 27, 1980 - Nov 27, 1981   11 - 12
  ② Oct 10, 1992 - Nov 10, 1993   23 - 24
  ③ Sept 24, 2004 - Oct 25, 2005   35 - 36
My Age: ④ Sept 19, 2016 - Oct 10, 2017   47 - 48

More precise date range of Jupiter return

____

(optional, referencing an ephemeris and +/- __3__ °orb, see
Appendix B)   1°55' ____ 4°55' ____ 7°55'
                   -3°   +3°

  ① Nov 7 - Dec 15, 1980
    Mar 7 - Apr 26, 1981
    Jun 29 - Aug 13, 1981

  ② Oct 20 - Nov 20, 1992
    Apr 14 - July 19, 1993

  ③ Oct 4 - Nov 2, 2004

  ④ Sept 18 - Oct 16, 2016

132

How Jupiterian Am I? Worksheet

Referring to your natal chart, let's see how strong your Jupiter signature is. This worksheet will also ask you to look for planets and placements you have in Sagittarius or Pisces, the two signs "ruled" by Jupiter and associated with strong Jupiterian energy.

	Yes	No
Jupiter in Sagittarius or Pisces		✓
Sun in Sagittarius or Pisces		✓
Moon in Sagittarius or Pisces		✓
Ascendant (ASC 12th/1st house cusp) in Sagittarius or Pisces	✓	
Midheaven (MC 9th/10th house cusp) in Sagittarius or Pisces	✓	
Three or more planets/ASC/MC (a stellium) in Sagittarius or Pisces		✓
Jupiter in aspect to the Sun, Moon, ASC or MC	✓	
Jupiter in the 1st house		✓
Sun, Moon or concentration of planets in the 9th or 12th house	✓	
Jupiter is part of a Stellium, Grand Trine, T-square, Grand Cross, Yod	✓	
Day Chart (Sun in 7-12 house)	✓	
Jupiter in Cancer		✓
Jupiter retrograde	✓	

Appendix E -- Extra Journal Pages